The HANDS and FEET of the HEART

The HANDS and FEET of the HEART

by Hisako Nakamura

BUDDHIST EDUCATION CENTER

MY FAVORITE FRIEND was my wordless doll. How I loved that doll sprawled on top of the chest of drawers...

She wore a dress made of cloth with a red checkered pattern. Her hair was luxurious and her round pupils looked like bells. But what caused me the most envy were her hands, each with four fingers and a thumb (even if they were a little thin), and two feet.

"How lucky you are to have both hands and feet!" I would say to my doll enviously. "Will you lend them to me...?"

—Hisako Nakamura's *Mukei no Te to Ashi* (Formless Hands and Feet)

I WISH I HAD A HAND with four fingers and a thumb...

Everyone taunts me. "Hand-less!" "Foot-less!" they shout.

Where are my hands? Where are my feet? Who took them away? I want them back...Please return them!

How clearly I remember the days and nights that I both screamed and cried like that.

But regardless of how I cried, not even a finger was returned to my body, much less a complete hand or foot.

I wonder if people blessed with two hands and two feet have ever considered what it is like to be without even one hand or one foot? And I wonder how many people appreciate their four fingers and thumb, and five toes by saying, "Thank you," to them?

How many times have I thought about this...

— Hisako Nakamura's *Muge no Michi* (*The Unimpeded Path*)

The doll presented to Helen Keller.

Table of Contents

Foreword

As related in the chapter titled, "Hisako Nakamura and Me," when I visited Mrs. Nakamura's grave (located in Takayama City, Gifu Prefecture, Japan), during September of 1980, I met her husband, Mr. Toshio Nakamura, and her second daughter, Tomiko, and reminisced with them at great length about the late Mrs. Nakamura.

After returning to the United States, I decided that I just had to introduce this remarkable woman to the English-speaking world. I felt however, that just translating Mrs. Nakamura's book, *Kokoro no Teashi* (The Hands and Feet of the Heart) directly into English might not be the best way to do so beause of the rather unorganized nature of that work. Accordingly, I selected parts of that work, articles that she wrote (including one that she wrote especially for the West Los Angeles Buddhist Temple's newsletter), and other writings, and edited them to form this work.

Because Mrs. Nakamura was of the older Japanese generation, her use of certain terms, and especially her reading of many *kanji* characters, makes her writing difficult for modern Japanese people to understand. I would like to thank Mr.

Nakamura and Tomiko for their great help in making difficult to understand parts of Mrs. Nakamura's text clear.

Since a large part of the text in this work was taken from *Kokoro no Teashi*, I decided to use the English equivalent for the title of this work. The illustration of Kwannon Bosatsu on page 74 of this book was drawn by Mrs. Nakamura by holding the pen in both of her limbs that are without hands.

❀

Last year, when my wife Shizuko underwent an operation for stomach cancer, her doctor discovered that the cancer had extended to her liver, and that she would not have much longer to live. Knowing me better than anyone else in this world, and knowing how much I wished to introduce Mrs. Nakamura to the English-speaking world, my wife urged me to use the *koden* from her funeral, her insurance and money from disposing of her beloved tea ceremony utensils, to publish this work. After much consideration, I decided to do as she asked. I believe publication of this work is a fitting memorial to my late wife.

If a single page or even a single word of this work inspires you to live a more Jodo Shinshu life, I am sure that my wife will take great joy in this from the Pure Land.

I would like to thank Mr. Ken'ichi Yokogawa for translating this work into English.

Finally, I would like to thank the Right Reverend Seigen Yamaoka, Socho of the BCA, for taking time from his busy schedule to write words of appreciation.

Bunyu Fujimura

Foreword

I would like to express my gratitude to the Orange County Buddhist Church Buddhist Education Center for reprinting *The Hands and Feet of the Heart*. Mrs. Hisako Nakamura's life has touched many people in Japan. Even today, her life story inspires many people in the United States and elsewhere. I have been one of them.

I was 9 years of age when I first encountered Mrs. Nakamura, who visited my home temple in Fukuoka to give a dharma talk. I still remember the day when a large crowd gathered at my temple and welcomed this famous lady without limbs. Since I was just a little boy, I was curious to see how she was able to get around. Does she walk? Does she roll around? To my surprise, it was neither. Mrs. Nakamura's husband carried her on his back. When she arrived, I could not help but notice the very nice and warm smile upon her face.

My home temple was packed with people who came from near and far to see Mrs. Nakamura with their own eyes and listen to what she had to say. I saw tears in everyone's eyes and heard the Nembutsu being recited from their mouths.

After her talk, she retired to the guest room, and I was invited into the room. At that time, Mrs. Nakamura decided to write a poem on a sheet of paper using a brush. She placed the brush in her mouth and started to write. I watched as she carefully wrote. Then she scolded me, "What's wrong with you!" It was almost a shout, and I did not know what was happening. She said, "You have healthy legs. Don't stand on your knees to watch me write. Sit square on the floor." I was so ashamed and embarrassed by her remarks.

Even now, I remember the incident vividly. I deeply thank her for her kindness of scolding me at that time. Mrs. Hisako Nakamura was an incredible lady, who lived and died with the Nembutsu. She had written the following on the sheet of paper:

Te wa nakumo,
Ashi wa nakutomo,
Mihotoke no
Sodenikurumaru,
Yasuki hi kana.

Although I have
no arms and legs,
how peaceful the day is
that I am being wrapped in
the Buddha's sleeves.

Mrs. Nakamura lived an unimaginably harsh life, yet she did not hate her life. Through her realization of being within the immeasurable life and light (Buddha's sleeves), she was able to live through her karmic life fully.

May readers of this book experience the heart of Mrs. Nakamura and be guided to the immeasurable life and light that ceaselessly embraces all sentient beings.

Rev. Kodo Umezu
Director, Center for Buddhist Education
Buddhist Churches of America

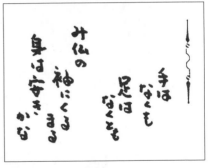

The calligraphy of Hisako Nakamura
was created by holding
the brush in her mouth.

Takayama City

Beginning of the Tragedy

TAKAYAMA CITY IS LOCATED in a valley surrounded by the Japan Alps. During winter, the temperature frequently falls 10 to 15 degrees below freezing. That is where I was born.

My father was a tatami-maker named Eitaro Kamanari, the successor of the Kamanari family. He was 33 years of age when I was born.

My mother was Aya Kamanari, the eldest daughter of the Maruano family, traditional doctors of herbology and external medicine. She was 27 years of age when she gave birth to me.

Autumn ends early on the high plains. Although fall was not even half over, the trees had already shed their leaves and the cold days that portended the coming winter continued.

"My feet...they hurt!" I cried.

Mother looked at me strangely when I cried like that. When she examined me, she discovered a purple spot about an inch and a half in diameter on my left instep. Thinking it was frostbite, she attended to it in the simplest way possible. But it did not become better the next day, or the next; rather, it grew worse. My parents finally took me to the hospital.

The doctors discovered that I had gangrene. "Both feet must be amputated. And since she is just a child, we cannot guarantee that she will survive the operation," they said.

I was the first child born to my parents after 11 years of marriage, so they must have wanted me very much. They begged the doctors to heal their only child without resorting to amputation, but my illness continued despite my parents' compassionate yearnings.

Now, not only my legs but both my arms became black with fever, and the pain in my limbs was with me day and night.

One day, when I cried out particularly violently, my mother came running out of the kitchen to see what was the matter. She found my bandaged left hand had fallen off at the wrist.

Mother fainted.

My right hand at my wrist, my left leg between my knee and foot, and my right foot, were all amputated to keep the gangrene from spreading.

"She may not last the night," the doctors frequently told my parents. "Be prepared to hold a funeral for her tomorrow."

How my parents must have wished a peaceful death for their beloved child.

By the time I reached my third birthday on November 25th, I had already become a pitiful figure of a child with neither hands nor feet.

But the pain continued.

By the time of the fall equinox, the flesh that was left on the stumps of my arms and legs cracked open like a pomegranate. My bones were exposed and caused much pain. I cried day and night.

"What a noisy child!" our neighbors grumbled.

They raised such a ruckus that after a winter, my family felt compelled to move out of the neighborhood. After that, my parents were forced to change their residence almost every year.

Forgetting about eating or sleeping, whether it rained, or whether the middle of the night; my parents and grandmother walked the streets carrying a child without hands or feet, so their neighbors would not be disturbed by its cries.

(Left to right)
Hisako's
grandmother,
and mother
Aya Kamanari

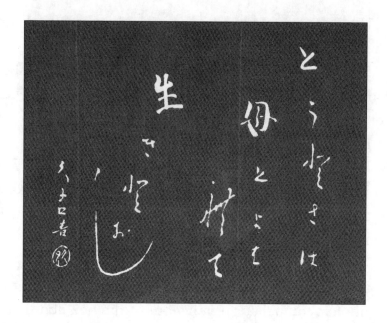

Examples of Mrs. Nakamura's calligraphy

Father's Death

"WHEN YOU WERE YOUNG, you broke your promise to marry the girl you loved. That is why your child had her hands and feet cut off.

But if you repent to the *kami* (god) with all your heart and make offerings, I guarantee that the pain in your child's arms and legs, and your suffering will disappear. Please rely on the kami with peace of mind!"

These were the words of the Tenrikyo religious leader my father was introduced to by a friend. I was told that my father took these words to heart. He sold our meager family belongings, and began spending all his time at the Tenrikyo meeting place.

The meeting place was actually just a room on the second floor of a rented house where a Shinto altar was enshrined.

Takayama City has a large Buddhist following. The majority of those Buddhists are followers of the Jodo Shinshu school of Buddhism, started by Shinran Shonin. Both my father's and mother's families were members of Jodo Shinshu temples.

Freedom of religious choice is taken for granted in Japan today. But in those days, it was not a simple matter for the head of a family to change his religion. A conference was held with all of the close relatives to discuss the matter. Those attending said they understood my father's suffering, from having to nurse his crying child day and night, but they could not allow the family religion that had been maintained for so many generations to be cast aside simply for that reason.

But my father refused to be bound by his relatives. In a desperate effort to save me from my suffering, he accepted the Tenrikyo religion, against their wishes.

Although he was extremely poor, my father would stop work for two or three hours at a time and pray before the kami. At noon and at night, without regard for the heavy snows, he sacrificed sleep to carry his child, who was always crying, to the Tenrikyo meeting place to help me overcome my intense pain.

I physically experienced the strength of my father's love. I will never be able to express sufficient gratitude for the depths of that great love.

The Tenrikyo minister prayed over my diseased limbs. He then wet a piece of paper with water that had been offered to the kami, and placed that paper over the part of my body in pain.

Placing a piece of cool wet paper over the burning stumps that remained of my arms and legs would temporarily lessen the pain, even without a kami's help.

That was obvious to anyone, but because of my father's blind faith and desire to see me well, he had lost all reason.

"My child's pain has stopped because of kami-sama's healing power!" father rejoiced. "How grateful I am!"

My father made his livelihood from a small tatami floor matting shop, and of course, he was not very well off. Added to this, he took days and nights off to care for me. Paying hospital bills, buying special food to nourish my body, and above all, the offerings of rice and money that he gave to Tenrikyo; all resulted in him falling deeper and deeper into debt.

But the pain in my arms and legs would not go away. When winter came with its intense cold, more of what remained of my arms and legs had to be amputated. Still, the pain remained.

My younger brother was born when I was 5 years. Boys are prized over girls in most Japanese families because they are the ones who continue the family line. But my father doted on me even after my brother was born. He would sit me in the straw from which he made his tatami, and tell and retell stories to keep me entertained.

My mother scolded me whenever I did something naughty, but my father never did.

I will never forget one night during the year I turned 7.

It was in the latter part of July. The Miya River was filled to overflowing from the rains that fell continuously day after day. The roar from the river that night was so loud we could not sleep.

I was lying in bed with my father. He gently shook me awake.

"Hisa-*chan*," he said softly, "I will never let you go. Even if I have to beg, even if I die, I will never let you go!"

He hugged me tightly.

I wondered what was wrong with my father, but even as I was wondering, he fell over on the futon bedding.

I became frightened and began to cry. My mother came running in to see what had happened. She raised my father to a sitting position. Regardless of how she shouted, however, my father did not reply. Neither her dedicated nursing nor the doctor's ministrations were of any avail. The Tenrikyo minister's prayers were, of course, more than useless.

Three days later, my father who loved me even to his death, left this world, a victim of cerebral meningitis. He was 39 years of age.

Later, I learned that the Tenrikyo minister told my mother, "This happened because your husband's repentance and offerings were inadequate."

I wondered what my still-young mother thought about this. She was left with a large debt, a daughter without hands or feet, and a 3-year-old son.

In later years, when I was forced to walk a similarly difficult road, I tasted the same tears that undoubtedly flowed down my mother's cheeks then. I was reminded of the difficulties that flow in the blood of a mother's body, and I cannot refrain from bowing my head in memory of my mother.

What a sad place home was without father…

How I yearned for him when the evening sun painted the trees in crimson and silently sank below the hills, and the lonely sound of the temple bell in Higashiyama could be heard.

When dusk turned to darkness, I was sure my father would come home. Although in vain, I could not help but listen for sounds of his return. Such days continued for a long time.

My grandmother occasionally came to visit when I was home by myself. How happy that made me! "Please stay with me all the time, Grandmother!" I continually badgered her, causing her much trouble and making her cry.

Although I was very lonely then, that was also a time when I was lovingly cared for by my mother and grand-mother, and therefore it was also a very fortunate time for me.

When the 49th-day memorial service was held for my father, the mountain peaks surrounding our town were again covered with snow, and the pain in my arms and legs returned.

Not knowing how to stop the pain in my limbs, my mother and grandmother alternated in carrying me on their back every night, walking the snow-packed streets of town, singing children's songs to amuse me. They walked the streets so my crying would not disturb our immediate neighbors.

The sound of a *geta* (wooden clog) being kicked against Kaji Bridge to remove the snow from the geta, all the while singing a lullaby in a soft voice to distract me… these are the memories of my mother and grandmother that remain deep within me even today.

Our relatives gathered almost every night to discuss my father's debts and what to do about my mother and the two children he had left behind. My mother became even more gaunt as a result of these discussions. In my childish innocence of what was going on, however, I thought only of the stimulation from the increased number of people who came to visit, and I was contentedly coddled on my uncle's knee.

It was finally decided that, because he was completely sound physically, my younger brother would be adopted by my uncle, the head of the Unehada family (my father's real family — he had been adopted into the Kamanari family), and mother and I would return to mother's family.

Mother's Remarriage

MOTHER'S FAMILY FOR MANY GENERATIONS had made its living as physicians, but my mother's younger brother had broken tradition and became a school teacher.

Although my mother was the elder sister of the head of that household, she was placed in a very difficult position. She had returned with a child who constantly cried in pain and did not have the money to pay my hospital fees.

For this reason, not long after returning to her family, my mother accepted the proposal of a widower named Fujita. One of the conditions of the marriage was that I could be brought along.

I was 8 years of age. I remember the snows were very deep then.

Mr. Fujita had a son the same age as myself and a daughter two years older. These were the children I was to call my new brother and sister.

My grandmother and other relatives were opposed to my mother's remarriage, but there was no way my mother could support us without marrying again. Mr. Fujita's family also opposed the marriage because of the inconvenience of a woman who brought a child without hands or feet.

I discovered how difficult life could be in a family where I was not wanted.

"Don't show your face outside the door!"

"A deformed child doesn't need an education!"

These were the things I was told by my step-father.

Everyone else goes to school, I thought. *Why am I alone not allowed to go? Why am I the only one without hands and feet...I wish I had hands with four fingers and a thumb... I wish I had legs on which I could walk... How happy I would be if I had these things...*These were the thoughts that continually filled my mind.

Immediately after my father's death, I was able to cajole my mother and grandmother into buying me whatever I wanted. Until my mother's remarriage, therefore, I was treated like a spoiled brat.

But all this changed when my mother married Mr. Fujita. Not only was my step-father cold towards me, my mother always took the side of her husband's children when a dispute arose between us children, and I would be the only one scolded. I always received the smallest piece of confectionery. And not only confectionery, but the smallest and least of everything.

My heart became dark and twisted as a result.

"Let's return to grandmother's home, please, I want to play with Eiji!" I would implore my mother, with tears in my eyes, whenever I was excluded from things.

"We no longer have a home that we can return to," my mother would tell me as gently as possible. "This is a very important place for us, so please be a good girl and remain silent."

But I would look resentfully at my mother whenever she said such things, bringing tears to her eyes.

Although she was against the remarriage, my grandmother realized there was no place for my mother and me other than with the Fujita family.

One clear night, when the moon was a thin crescent, high in the sky and the cold turned our breath to ice...

"Hisa-*chan*, Hisa-*chan*."

Someone was calling me from outside in a low voice. When I crawled to the door and looked out through a crack, I saw my beloved grandmother's face wrapped in a cloth hat.

"Oh, *Oba-sama!*," I said happily.

"They walked the streets so my crying would not disturb our immediate neighbors."

"I think about you all the time," she said. "I want to see and talk with you, but unfortunately, I cannot come to this house for the time being. When I am allowed to come, I will come every day, if possible, so please be patient and play with your step-brother and step-sister until then...alright? You understand, don't you? Please stop crying...Here, I brought you a toy."

Grandmother often came to visit me secretly like that, against the wishes of my uncle.

What a sad, pitiful karma that my grandmother, mother, step-father, step-brother, and step-sister had...

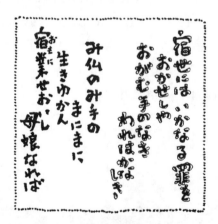

Calligraphy by
Mrs. Nakamura

Losing the Light

THE CLOUDS OF WAR between Japan and Russia cleared, and spring arrived again. On the 15th day of April, a festival was to be held at Hiei Shrine. The spirits of the people were revived after a long winter, and everyone eagerly looked forward to the warmer days.

My eyes began hurting that night. By the next morning, I couldn't see anything. Everything was completely dark. I could not see my mother's face, the people in our house, or anything in the room. In the space of one night, both of my eyes were completely shut out from the light of the world.

My mother was unable to contain herself and cried out loudly. All I could hear in the complete darkness was my mother's wailing voice.

My mother and grandmother brought me to the hospital. The doctor said the pain in my arms and legs had affected my eyes, and therefore, recovery from my loss of sight was uncertain.

Being burdened with a 9-year-old daughter who was blind, in addition to not having hands or feet, was almost too much for my mother.

My aunt, who was caring for my younger brother Eiji, had passed away in January of that year. She left three children of her own, in addition to Eiji. My mother's relatives gathered to decide what to do about my brother. After much discussion, they decided to place him in an orphanage. Consequently, my younger brother, who was then only 5 years of age, and as the eldest son, should have been the center of attention on Boy's Day, May 5th, was instead led by a complete stranger over a mountain to an orphanage in the town of Kano.

Tears flowed from my eyes that were incapable of seeing anything.

"What an inhuman mother! She didn't even see her own child being placed in the custody of another. She must not care for him at all!"

"She gave birth to him, but she didn't even see him off. What a terrible mother."

That is how my aunts on my father's side abused my mother, who did not see my little brother off to the orphanage.

The night before, however, carrying me on her back and muffling the sound of her feet as much as possible, my mother loitered for hours in front of the house where her beloved son was spending his last night.

My mother listened intently from outside the house for the voice of her innocent child who didn't know his own fate—who knows the mind of such a pitiful mother? She finally left dejectedly about midnight with her neck sunk deep into her collar.

"*Kaka-sama*, where are you going?" I asked.

My mother didn't answer. She just walked on weakly. Finally, she said in a sad voice, "Would you like to go to a nice place with mommy?"

Mother's geta pressing down on the pebbles on the road made a lonely sound. In the silence of the night, mother and child seemed to be drawn by a string pulled by a ghost. She staggered step by step into the darkness.

The night wind blew through the trees, swaying the tops, making a ghastly sound, and then passed on. Fraught with fear, I clung to my mother's back with the stumps of my arms.

"Hisa-*chan*, please forgive me..."

Cold tears from my mother's eyes fell on my cheeks when she turned her head to look back at me.

Without knowing why, I felt sad and cried. Mother said something soothing, and trudged along.

Where was my mother going?

Although summer had almost arrived, and green leaves were just beginning to show their buds, the nights on the Hida Plain were still chilly. The cold of winter that still remained seeped into our bodies.

My mother seemed to have finally reached her destination. The roar of the water could be heard just in front of us.

A waterfall.

We were southeast of town, where the Miya River makes a spectacular drop. My mother did not move. She just stood there for a long time. Fear hardened in me, like the night dew solidifying to ice on my shivering body...

"Mommy, I'm scared...!"

Mother didn't stir. Her mind seemed to be far off somewhere else.

The sound of the water, that made me think of the bottom of hell, shook the earth incessantly where mother stood.

"Don't cry," my mother said, finally. "It's alright... let's return home..." She sighed slightly, and began staggering weakly back the way she had come.

Was there a more unfortunate mother and child? How difficult to continue living.

Poor mother.

I existed for more than half a year in complete darkness.

"It may be impossible to reattach the hands and feet that were amputated, but I would like to at least let her eyes recognize the light of the sun again"...That was all my grandmother thought about. She encouraged my mother, who had fallen into the depths of despair, and it was my grandmother who brought me to Kawakami Hospital.

When fresh snow began to decorate the top of the

ginkgo tree in Kokubun Temple, I gradually began to make out the square-shaped skylight, and even the lattice. The joy I felt at again being able to recognize the light is something that I will never forget. How much I owe mother's and grandmother's earnest efforts, and the dedication with which the staff of Kawakami Hospital nursed me.

And that is how I learned what it is like to be blind. Heaven gave me a great opportunity to experience what it is like to be unable to see.

Top: Takeyama City,
Bottom: Temple where Hisako listed to the dharma.

Nembutsu is real and true. From The *Tannisho,*
Shinran Shonin. Calligraphy by Hisako at age 69.

Education

I WAS 10 YEARS OF AGE when I received the texts, readers, and books on *shushin* (moral training, which is no longer taught in Japan) that my step-brother had used.

Grandmother bought me paper, pencils, slate and chalk, and other necessities for studying. I copied what my step-brother and step-sister wrote, and gradually began to gain the rudiments of an education. I began writing by holding pencils and chalk in my mouth.

I don't remember when or how I began, but at some point, I began using scissors with my legs.

When the rainy season arrived, mother told me to remake the clothes that had become worn during the cold winter months. She told me what I should unravel. I could not cut the sturdy thread used to sew the cuff, sleeve attachment, and the edge of the collar, with my legs; so I asked my mother to cut it for me. She said I should figure out a way to cut it myself, and left me alone with a pile of clothing.

After a great deal of effort, I finally realized that I could use the scissors with my mouth to cut the thread. I could unravel old clothes by myself! That was one of my great discoveries, and a source of great joy.

"Using a needle is a woman's most important ability. If only I could teach you to sew."

My heart trembled at this statement by my mother. "That's it," I decided... and the thought of my favorite doll with the red *yuzen* (a type of fabric dying) garment that grandmother made for me. I was determined to practice holding a needle in my mouth and sew a garment for it.

After much effort, I was finally able to handle a needle, but I could not thread it. I would ask my mother or grandmother, or my step-sister; but as often as not, they would be busy just when I wanted my needle threaded.

I tried even harder. And miracle of miracles, I was finally able to thread a needle by myself! But whatever I sewed, whether it was bean bags, a purse, or clothes for my beloved doll, I had to smooth the stitches and make the creases with my mouth. Accordingly, everything was wet with my saliva and had to be dried by the fire. But the fact that I could sew by myself was a source of great joy that I cannot begin to describe.

But then I began to notice my step-sister and friends in the neighborhood would knit and crochet as well; and this made me envious. I saw their fingers move quickly back and forth in doing this work, and so I wanted to knit, too.

I thought and thought about how I could do it, and finally succeeded. But learning to knit was not accomplished after just a morning or evening of trying.

Even striking a match was a struggle. I was unable to do so at first, so I asked my mother to do it for me. As usual, however, she told me to do it myself.

After thinking about it for a long time, I finally hit on the strategy of placing the matchstick in the mouthpiece of a *kiseru*, a Japanese tobacco pipe. A kiseru is different from western-style pipes in that it holds just enough tobacco for one or two puffs. At any rate, I placed the matchstick in the mouthpiece. The larger holding area allowed me to grasp the kiseru with my limbs sufficiently to strike the match. But the fire extinguished when it reached the metal part of the mouthpiece. I kept stuffing more matches into the mouthpiece and striking matches until mother felt I was wasting matches. She took the kiseru pipe away from me and placed it up high where I could not reach it. How angry I was at my mother for doing that! I even went so far as to wonder if I was her real daughter or whether she was treating me that way because I was a step-daughter.

It may sound as though my mother treated me very coldly, but actually, it was only because she treated me as she did that I was finally able to care for most of my personal needs by myself.

Perhaps it sounds as if everything came easily to me once I figured out how to do it, and that I did not have any difficulty doing things. But actually, there were many things that I could not do, and I cannot begin to describe

how difficult it was to do even the simplest of tasks.

My sewing...I was very proud that I could sew, even if the result was always wet with my saliva. Once, I was overjoyed when a friend asked me to sew a dress for her doll. I was extremely proud of the result of my hand-iwork, but my friend's mother took one look at what I had created, and saying she would not have such a dirty thing in her house, threw it into a nearby stream.

When I later heard what had happened to the dress that I was so proud of, I finally realized what it meant to not have hands. Although I still cried from the pain in my limbs when winter came every year, until then I had not understood what a hindrance it was to not have hands.

I could not forget the doll's dress that I had sewn was thrown out. *Everything I sew will be wet with saliva if I sew with my mouth*, I thought, *so how about using the stumps of my legs?*

I was determined to learn to sew with my legs. But the limbs of my legs did not have toes with which to hold a needle. When I realized I did not have hands or feet, everything became black, and I could only cry.

Why does everyone else have hands and feet and only I don't? The more I thought about it, the more the joy of creating things, and even the desire to do so, disappeared.

Eventually, however, I remembered how much I enjoyed

sewing, and gradually took up a needle again. But always in the back of my mind was the desire not to slobber over what I was making, not to let what I was making get wet. I continued my pathetic efforts in sewing with this thought in my mind. The fact that the dress I made for my friend's doll had been thrown away became the impetus for me to concentrate even harder. When I was sewing, therefore, I went into a *samadhi*-like meditative state.

But it was 13 years before I could finally sew without dribbling over what I was working on. With the passing of years, however, my teeth have weakened, and I am no longer able to sew or knit.

"How much better if you could eat by yourself."

Spring arrived, then winter, and then spring again, but regardless of how much time passed, my mother always had to feed me my three meals a day. Because she also had to care for me, my mother was even more hard-pressed to serve her husband when we had guests.

"Let's think of a way you can eat by yourself."

Although I wanted to feed myself very badly, the fact remained that I did not have fingers with which to hold chopsticks. No matter how I considered it, I could not think of a way to hold an *ochawan* (rice bowl), or *ohashi* (chopsticks). All I could do was place the plate holding the food on a low tray, and gobble the food with my mouth. Crude as it was, eating by myself like that, rather than being fed, made the food tastier. I even considered it

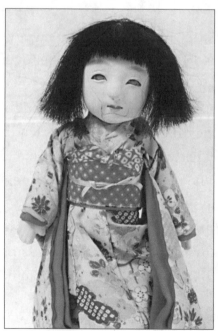

to be a new discovery. When the boy next door laughed at me, however, saying, "People who don't eat with chopsticks are no better than dogs or cats," I was suddenly brought to reconsider my way of eating. Seeing the sad look on my mother's face when she heard the neighborhood children talk about me like that, I deter-

mined in that moment, I am not like a dog or a cat! Even if I don't have hands or feet, I am a human being! I'll show those kids that I can eat with chopsticks...somehow or other, I'm going to do it! This fierce determination, plus the rebellious spirit of my childhood, burned within me. After much trial and error, I was finally able to grasp both chopsticks and a rice bowl in the stumps that remained of my arms and use them to feed myself. Being told that I was "just like a dog or a cat," was the impetus that allowed me to escape being associated with animals.

Hisako and dolls she made.

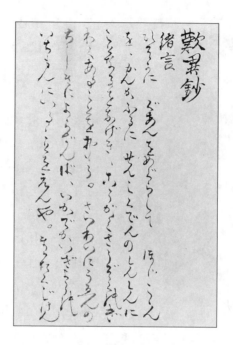

Examples of Hisako's calligraphy

Mother's Suffering

MY STEPFATHER DID NOT like to have a disabled child like me around. He was embarrassed to have strangers see me, so I was forced to spend all my time in a room on the second floor.

As a result, I could not go to the toilet when I wanted. There were times when I had to bear it for three and even five hours before I could relieve myself. This was more difficult for me to bear, and a source of far greater sorrow than having to wait for meals.

Mother rose before anyone else every morning. She then woke me, took me to the toilet, washed my face, dressed me, and rewrapped all the bandages on my arms and legs. This took at least an hour. I was then placed back in bed until it was time for breakfast.

Mother and my step-father quarrelled about me constantly, causing me much distress. But it was undoubtedly much more trying for mother. Just bringing me to the doctor during the winter, when my pain was most intense, was extremely difficult for her.

As a girl, I wanted to wear clothes with bright, attrac-

tive colors, but I was never allowed to. All I had was clothing made of hand-woven cotton, made in the same style as
worn by my step-brother. As a result, I was always laughed
at by friends. This caused me much shame. Later, when
I was older, my mother bought me an *obi* sash made of
muslin with a red bamboo design. That made me very happy, but even to our family we said grandmother bought it
for me.

The combined responsibility of caring for me and her
second husband's household, left mother without even a
moment to herself. As a result, she finally left her second
husband's home.

The life that mother and I led after she left her second
husband was a very poverty-stricken one, but for me it
was extremely pleasant because I could be so much more
at ease. Mother worked in a silk-spinning mill and grandmother took care of the household chores while she was
away, and of course, cared for me. When we had a visitor,
there was no need to hide me in the back or in a closet.
That may not seem like much to most people, but for me,
it was as if the heaven and earth had opened up.

But what made me happiest about the arrangement
was that I could be taken to the toilet whenever I wanted.

When fall came around that same year, when the trees
in the mountains shed their leaves and I began to feel the
pain in my arms and legs again, mother returned to her
second husband's home.

The less than one year that we lived apart from my

step-father was like heaven to me, and because of that taste of freedom, my step-father's home became an even more difficult place for me to live.

"Let's return to our home next to the river. Please bring me to grandmother's home..." I cried and pleaded with mother. But to no avail. Mother found it impossible to live without the support of a male.

At that age I could not begin to fathom mother's feelings, and only felt sorry for myself at being returned to my step-father's house. How I resented mother then. When I think about it now, however, I realize the great burden I was for her.

The upstairs room that was given to me was where both mother and daughter suffered.

Once during the rainy season, mother left me in grandmother's care and went to work in a silk-spinning mill in Shimosuwa in Shin Province. Why did my physically frail mother walk a distance of 30 miles over mountains and through valleys? Even in my childish mind I thought it strange. Later, I learned that she was forced to earn extra money to pay for the hospitalization I required because of the pain in my arms and legs that recurred every year.

"Mommy, please forgive me..." I apologized in my heart. The suffering that mother endured for my sake was not the usual sort that most mothers are subjected to.

I was supported by mother's strong love for me and because grandmother, who took great joy in the Nembutsu, was always there to console me when my pain was the strongest.

Sumie Brush painting,
the only artwork remaining.

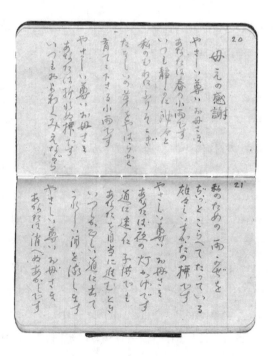

Expressing appreciation to her
mother in her diary.

The Only Way Open

DO DON KO. DON, DON. BOOM, BOOM. In Japan, the
sound of *taiko* drums is associated with the Obon festival,
a time of reflection for our loved ones who have preceded
us in leaving this world.

The sounds of the Obon festival are always carried on
the evening breeze at the beginning of autumn. When I
was a child, my father was often asked to perform the
shamisen (a string instrument) during the Obon festivi-
ties. He always brought me with him. When our relatives
would make a face and ask the propriety of bringing a
deformed child to the Obon festival, my father would always reply, "I'm bringing her because she's deformed!
Who will bring her if her own father won't?!"

When the Obon season arrived during September, every year my longing for my father always increased. With
the passing years, I remembered my father, who is now
sleeping in a grave on Mt. Gobo, even more fondly.

Whenever I heard about the death of someone I knew,
I wondered why I did not die. I began to await my death.
was because I knew that my frail and sickly mother would

suffer as long as I was alive. I began to feel that things would be much easier for my family if I was no longer a part of it.

"That child is still alive...it's probably because someone cast a curse on her, which is why that handless and footless person is still living."

These cold words by cold-hearted people in town hurt my mother both physically and mentally, and were the cause of even more discord in the family.

And I could not forget that the cause of that discord was this "bothersome, burdensome person." If only I could die!

The fact that a person without hands and feet was still alive was not something to be happy about, nor something that brought comfort to those around her. What continued to pass through my mind 24 hours of every day was "death."

Even during that period, the Japanese government provided a small amount of financial aid for the poor and destitute, and those who were handicapped. My mother often considered applying for such assistance. In my case, however, there was no telling how long I could receive such aid before I could become self-supporting. And because the money would be from the country of Japan, and in a higher sense, from the Emperor of Japan himself, it weighed upon me even more.

I was a bother to the city of Takayama because I did not contribute even the slightest bit. I was, thus, completely unworthy of receiving an allowance. For that reason, I firmly decided that as long as I was going to continue living, I would support myself, even if I did not have hands or feet.

One summer evening, an old friend of my late father came to visit. I had a premonition of something important the moment he entered my room.

"I am worried about your future now that you are becoming an adult," he began slowly. "Please don't misunderstand, and listen carefully to what I say. I am not in any way looking down on you, or holding you in contempt. I am only thinking of your future."

With tears in his eyes, he suggested working in a freak show for several years and saving all the money I made. With that as capital, he said, I would be able to buy a small store, hire a maid, and support myself. If I did that, he said, I would not be a burden on my relatives in my old age.

I considered this proposition day and night.

When my father was alive, freak shows were always held on the banks of the Miya River during festival times. When a show manager heard about me, he would come to my father and say, "I will give you all the money you want. Please let me adopt your daughter and let her work in my show. If that doesn't appeal to you, then please let her work for me just a short while…"

But my father was adamant, rejecting all such requests.

"We may be poor," he would reply sternly, "but I will not sell my child just so I can eat!"

I heard about my father's attitude regarding this many times, both from my mother and grandmother. For that reason, I had determined that regardless of how much I suffered, I would not be put on exhibition in a freak show. How could I apologize to my late father if I did?

Further, even if I had neither hands nor feet, I had my pride as a young woman. I cannot fall so low as to be

exhibited as a freak, I thought. I must not lose my self-respect, I told myself severely.

But another part of me criticized this feeling. What else is there that I can do to make a living?

How else can I support myself?

Should I allow myself to be exhibited as a freak or not?

Hisako, age 24.

Freak Show

"YOU ARE, AFTER ALL, burdened with a handicapped body. If you have even the least bit of difficulty, please feel free to return home immediately... and please, take good care of yourself."

That was what my mother had told me as I was leaving, her voice wet with tears. I was filled with emotion and could not say a word. I could only nod my head.

When the time finally came, I hated leaving my step-father's house, even though it was not a place where I could truly relax. How much more, then, did I hate leaving my step-brother, who had quietly protected me.

It was hard to tell my grandmother what I had decided to do. I finally informed her indirectly, by asking her to order me a *haori* (light coat) woven from a silk fabric. When I requested this of her, she, (like any Japanese person), immediately realized that I would be leaving. And because of the many discussions she had participated in regarding my future, she also knew that I could only be going to a freak show. With this haori clutched firmly within the limbs of my arms, I took my leave.

I was then 20 years of age and would not have been able to exist for even a single day without my mother or my grandmother. Now I was leaving those who were closest and dearest to me, and to whom I owed the greatest of debts. I was placed in the hands of people whom I had never met before. I wondered how my mother felt about having to give up her handless and footless daughter to strangers.

Late autumn in the mountain provinces changed to winter. The chilly wind in the middle of the night blew the leaves from the trees. The Milky Way drifted coldly in the clear sky.

November 6, 1916...

It was decided that, in order to avoid being seen, I would take the road behind the village of Hide to the freak show. I sat on a futon blanket in a cart, wedged between my wicker trunk containing two or three changes of clothing, and Mr. Kinoshita, nicknamed Ise-Kane, who was my father's friend. On my lap, I held a cloth pouch containing *omusubi* (rice ball), Japanese confectionery, toilet tissue, and other things my mother had packed for me. My mother came to see me off.

We reached the city of Nagoya on the evening of the fourth day. Nagoya is a large city, with many more people than would come out for the annual San-oh Festival in Takayama. I gasped when I saw the nightless city of Nagoya. Ise-Kane laughed at my naivety.

On December 1st, I was put on exhibition behind Osu

Temple by the Takaraza group. I was billed as *Daruma Musume*, the "Daruma Daughter."[2]

The day before, signs advertising the show were posted all over the city.

The day for my "debut" finally arrived. The name Daruma Musume might be said to be the fate of a woman without hands or feet. It was a name I hated.

"Welcome to our show," those who came to welcome me said in their thick Osaka accents and with newly-purchased happi coats. And that is how, whether I wanted to or not, I became an "artist" in their freak show.

As to my "art," I did needlework, knitted, and such things as tying knots. In addition, I did calligraphy.

That month, during a period when (strangely for Nagoya) the rain came down in sheets, I heard a male voice from the cheap section of the audience where the spectators had to stand: "Would you brush this, too?"

I looked at the piece of paper that was handed to me by an assistant. On it was written, "*Seishin itto nai goto ga narazaran* (All things are possible when the mind is concentrated)."

I was astonished by the magnificent strokes with which the characters were brushed, and furtively raised my eyes to peek at the person who made the request. He was a handsome young man about 21 or 22 years of age.

---

2 A "daruma" is a popular doll in Japan that comes from the legendary founder of Zen Buddhism, Bodhidharma. Bodhidharma is said to have meditated so long that his legs fell off, thus the dharuma doll has no legs.

He wore a dark blue kimono with a pattern of white splashes, on top of which he wore a mantle or cloak.

I don't know whether it was because I was shy, whether I still suffered from stage fright, or if it was because I was so unlearned, but I could not bring myself to copy the words on that sheet of paper. I declined as politely as I could several times, but the young man would not take "no" for an answer.

Finally he said, "It doesn't matter if the words are clumsily written." So, I was forced to take the brush in my mouth and brush the words. It was a cold day, but I felt the perspiration flowing from my armpits.

The next morning, the young man was waiting for me in front of the show entrance. He had a one-page model of Chinese characters, called a *te-hon*, paper, brush, sumi block, sumi stone, and all the implements to brush calligraphy. That young man was later to become the great calligraphy master, Roppo Oki.

"Even if you are in a freak show," he said, "you must be like a lotus growing in a muddy pond. You must develop the strength to not allow the mud to stain your spirit; otherwise, you cannot be called a human being."

I was later separated from kind "Uncle" Ise-Kane, and was handed over to the Kogyo-shi group, who were much stricter with me. I spent years with them, experiencing things that caused me to shed many tears. Young Roppo Oki's words sustained me during that difficult period.

During February of the following year, Uncle Ise-Kane

became the manager of our show and led our group outside Nagoya to Kyoto, Kobe, Fukui, Kanazawa, and many other places.

During our days off, Uncle Ise-Kane would place me in a cart and bring me to the scenic and well-known places where we were "performing."

Uncle Ise-Kane bought me my first kimono. And not just one. He bought me several, all made with silk or silk crepe. He treated me like his own daughter. He taught me how to use the *soroban* (abacus), how to write letters, and because he said it was important to understand and appreciate the tea ceremony, he taught me the rudiments of that art.

I adored Uncle Ise-Kane as if he were the incarnation of my father.

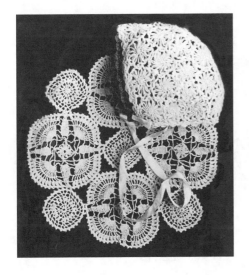

Hisako made crocheted hats and doilies.

Hisako (age 30) was a freak
show "artist" for 26 years.

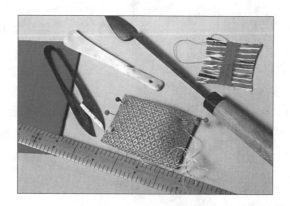

Sewing items Hisako used to
make Japanese dolls.

Love

WHILE I WAS LIVING AT HOME, I could not even think of the word, "love," let alone say it aloud.

But that does not mean I was unconcerned or unaware of love. Mere existence is not all there is to life. I began to understand how extremely important love is. I learned that having your heart shaken to its foundation is absolutely not a trivial thing.

Like a floating weed, drifting this way and that, a love developed in which both parties loved the other — even before they were aware of it.

He was a worker in the entertainment industry from the Kanto region (greater Tokyo area). He had lost both his parents and had neither brothers nor sisters. He was then about 23 or 24 years of age. His name was Yoshifuji.

He liked to drink and gamble more than eating. He was the ideal, if that is the word, of a *yakuza*, a Japanese gangster. But the yakuza have their ideals too; although they may not be the same as those of the populace in general, and Yoshifuji certainly lived up to them. He was the best "barker" in the Kanto region, and he always took the side of the weak and those who were honest. He was what is called in our entertainment world, a *ni-mime-gata-yakuza*, a gangster who is the love-making actor type. He fit in perfectly in any freak show.

"If your contract is for a year, then I'll wait for you," he said. "I have to be honest and confess that I will continue drinking, but I promise that if we get married, I will not drink so much that it will cause you concern. Please, believe me. Let's, the two of us, start our own small show and work as hard as we can. And let's go to Takayama City in Hide, too… Come on…marry me…please?"

Can you imagine how happy this made me? My heart shook from the very bottom of my being. A bright world that was completely unknown to me opened up.

Because of the long hours and close scrutiny by the spectators, it was difficult for me to perform my "act," but when it was over, I was overjoyed to be able to be with him. The other girls in the show, including the other handicapped young girl, were also attracted to Yoshifuji, but he did not so much as look at them. Just knowing that became a source of great pride for me.

"My, you seem exceptionally happy today, Hisa-*chan*…Oh, I see…" the members of the show would tell us with a sly smile.

That was how they teased us when they saw both his face and mine as he helped me, knowing full well what was developing between us.

When I was thirsty, I would never ask one of the

other young men who were assigned to assist me. Water from their hands was bland, but water from his was like nectar.

"Falling in love is like embracing the sun." I even went so far as to write nonsense like that in a letter to a friend.

For me, this living human being, who was unlikely to be accepted in normal society; this was like a warm nursery that cradled me as an individual for the first time, or rather, for the first time as a "woman."

Even in difficult circumstances that choked me and kept me from breathing, it was always young Yoshifuji who warmed my heart and added light to my life.

That was also about the time I began buying copies of the classics, such as *Manyo-shu* (*Collection of Ten Thousand Leaves*) and *Kokin-shu* (*Collection of Poems Old and New*) at night book stalls and studied them as much as I could between performances.

Regardless of how restricted life is, a fresh new world opens up if we do not consider our minds to be bound. And when I recall the man of my heart at that time, I cannot help feeling grateful at being surrounded by joy, and the light that made life worth living.

How happy is the handicapped person, who receives the great spiritual power from heaven, to overcome his or her physical handicap.

Hisako with her
calligraphy teacher.

Calligraphy by
Mrs. Nakamura

The Deaths of My Brother and Mother

"LITTLE BROTHER EIZO, where are you?

This thought has never left me for even a moment. Although I had agreed to throw my body away in a freak show, the one request I had of life was to find my little brother, whom I had lost track of, and return with him to my mother and grandmother, as brother and sister.

Regardless of how much suffering or sadness I was confronted by, I felt the responsibility to endure until I found my brother.

It was about the middle of December, when tiny flakes of snow began dancing down from the sky, that the *Ho-onko* (Shinran Shonin's Memorial) Service for the entertainment industry was held at the Ogaki City Buddhist Temple.

An old man came to see me. "Do you have a younger brother named Eizo Kamanari?" he asked.

I was astonished.

"I am his sister!" I replied excitedly. "Where did you meet my younger brother?"

The old man's name was Takahashi. He said he had

helped look after my brother while employed at Kano Orphanage. Mr. Takahashi told me that Eizo was presently apprenticed to a shop called Iwase Cleaning, located in Aoki City in Kanagawa Prefecture.

Mr. Takahashi told me all about my brother, and this made me so happy, I shed tears of joy.

Heaven has not discarded me, I thought. "Thank you for surviving until today, Eizo."

I immediately wrote to my brother. In the pitiful, melancholy letters that I received in reply, Eizo wrote, "We are brother and sister, who have not been of much help to each other. When I become an adult, I will look after you, so please bear it for just a little longer."

"Thank you, Eizo-*chan*. *Arigato*, thank you." How many times have I read his words through tear-dimmed eyes.

"If only *oto-sama*, our honorable father, were still alive. Then we could live happily together as brother and sister, like all other children."

With resentment and also sorrow, his words oozed with the feeling that he found misfortune in life, and that he too had been forced to walk a difficult road.

But how lucky I was to have endured… ah, how *arigatai* (grateful)… I wish I could see him as an adult, just once. And how I would like to let him meet our mother and grandmother again.

The fact that my brother was still alive…this caused a light—very much like a brilliant summer sun—to be poured all over me.

Four years later—May 14th of 1920— I received a telegram in the middle of the night:

EIZO SERIOUSLY ILL. COME IMMEDIATELY.

I felt as if I had been knocked to the ground. Thinking it was just a nightmare, I looked around, but I was not dreaming. It was real.

What happened? In the letter that I had received just a few days previously, Eizo said he was well and working hard. At any rate, I had to see him at least once, if for no other reason than to apologize. I felt I had to take our mother's place during Eizo's last moments. How could I face him in the Pure Land if I didn't? Poor Eizo... time passed unforgivingly, moment by moment, while he neared his end. Knowing this, I could not settle down.

"What are you going to do for money?" asked the young attendant, Nakatani, who Uncle Ise-Kane had assigned to me. I had no savings.

We went to Toyohashi City, where the head of the group I was then associated with had gone, and had the terms of my contract extended another six months. As a result, I was able to borrow 50 yen.

When Nakatani and I arrived at the Kanagawa train station, it was already past 9 o'clock in the evening. The May rain, as thin as threads, fell without a sound on my body. How lonely I felt. I kept praying for my brother's life all the way to Aoki City.

"He has meningitis. The doctors can do no more for him."

When I first heard those words, everything turned black in front of my eyes. But just knowing that a flicker of life remained in Eizo's body was a source of great comfort to me.

In Room 12 on the second floor, a young man was hovering unconsciously between life and death — he was my younger brother, whom I had sought for so many years...

"Eizo-chan, it's your sister! It's Hisa, Eizo, it's me. Do you remember...?"

But how could I have expected him to respond to my voice that was so filled with tears? How could I expect him to remember me when we had parted as such young children? He just lay there, groaning in pain. His face was flushed and both eyes were so swollen, I could not even make out the shape of his face.

"*O-kasan*, where is o-kasan... I can't see anything! O-kasan, open my eyes for me...please!"

My brother's voice calling for our mother made my heart feel as if it were breaking. Even as he lay dying, Eizo's thoughts were directed toward our mother... A mother is, after all, where our hearts all return.

Several extremely sad days passed. They were even sadder because Eizo did not respond to my voice which, because we had parted so long ago, he had completely forgotten.

How angry I was when the man my brother was

apprenticed to asked me to pay the doctor and medical bills. I hated the cold, merciless world and the people living in it. I considered dying then and there with my brother.

All there was from our mother in Takayama was a telegram stating that she could not come because of illness.

And then I received a telegram from the freak show:

COME TO IRAGOE IMMEDIATELY.

How I resented the words of that telegram. I wanted to stay with my brother for five or six more days. I wanted to at least be at his side when he drew his last breath. Once Eizo became aware that I was at his side, even if he could not see me, he would not let me leave for even a moment. How he would mourn if I were to leave. And how he would resent me for being such a cold and unfeeling sister.

I didn't want to leave. How much better it would be if both my body and heart just melted into nothingness.

It is the practice in the entertainment industry that if a performer is given an advance on his or her salary, to not let that performer get by for even a day without working.

I had to leave eight days after my arrival.

"*O-nesan*, don't leave me all alone! Please, stay with me... please o-nesan...!"

Chewing the sleeves of my kimono with anxiety, I left the hospital with these words of my brother still ringing in my ears.

Regardless of how long I live, I will not be able to erase the feeling of helplessness and sorrow.

EIZO DIED.

That was expected, of course, but still, it was just too sad. When I received that telegram, both my body and heart felt torn apart. I felt there was no longer any reason to live.

In his short 20 years of life, filled from beginning to end with tears, Eizo's earthly life was filled with sadness.

Please sleep in peace forever, protected by the Buddha in the Pure Land.

We performed in Hokkaido Prefecture for several months. With our final performance in Hakodate City, the thought of returning to the main island of Honshu was something that we all looked forward to, whether we had a home to return to or not, like myself. Just as I was having such thoughts, I received a long letter from my grandmother. I had not heard from her for a long time. Her letter contained news of my mother's passing.

My mother has passed away... was there ever so unfilial a child as I? How could I make amends?

Please forgive me, mother. In spite of having a child with neither hands nor feet, having to bear the scorn of the world, and having to marry into a cold family for my sake, you raised me well. It was only because of kakasama that I was able to continue living. I will continue to live life strongly because of you, kaka-sama.

Please find peace in the Pure Land.

My beloved kaka-sama.

In the short time between May and August, I lost two people most precious to me. I just sat in bleak amazement in my lodging by the harbor, listening to the rain falling softly.

What sad memories...
I will never forget the ravaging sea
Of Tsugaru Straits
In this northern prefecture
That I see now...
Wanting to disappear
Into the mist.

Mushin (egolessness)
Calligraphy by Mrs. Nakamura

Marriage

THE TIME FOR MARRIAGE came even for me. The person selected to be my husband was a young man named Yuzo Nakatani. He had accompanied me when I visited my dying brother, Eizo.

"Please take my place in caring for her," Uncle Ise-Kane pleaded with Nakatani. "A promise man to man."

Nakatani took the place of my hands and feet for several years, and cared for all my needs. In spite of his patience with me, however, I was short tempered with him, and did not respond towards him with love at all.

I just allowed myself to be taken care of by him. Boss Kishini was the *Nakodo*, (the go-between) and arranged everything. But Nakatani was not the man I loved. Spend my entire life with him? I thought about that a great deal. How I wished I at least had feet. I would not have married him if I had been able to walk by myself. But I could do almost nothing in my daily life without Nakatani's help. Starting with washing clothes, going to and from the stage for my performances, every aspect of my life required assistance from someone.

I went so far as to consult a friend in Nagoya.

"A good-looking man will just discard you someday, and you will only end up crying," she said. "Besides, few men are as kind and gentle as Yuzo ... I think you should consider the state of your body and endure it as best as you can."

The beautiful light of love shook my heart, faint though it might be. Thinking it through again and again, and while resenting the incompleteness of my body, I finally agreed to do as everyone urged.

❀

He was born in a village named Hagui on the Noto Peninsula, and was as honest and straight-forward a person as there is. He did not marry me out of pity or curiosity, but rather, from true understanding, deep sympathy, and his pure heart.

No one rejoiced more than my grandmother over the fact that a woman without hands and feet was able to marry.

Even with a body like this, I am allowed to live a married life. With gratitude, keenly aware of the value of living, I settled down to married life.

"Does it have hands and feet? And fingers and toes? And its head isn't too large, is it? "

Those were my first words after giving birth to a child.

"Yes, yes ... it's a fine baby girl with fully developed arms and legs. And its head is not excessively large."

The tiny infant that continued breathing quietly had two

arms and two legs. At the end of the arms were four fingers and a thumb, and at the end of the legs were five toes. And the beautiful pink-colored skin! What a magnificent gift had been given to me!

I will bear any suffering for the benefit of this child, I vowed. I will live strongly for her sake. After all, I am now a mother. I could not stop the tears of gratitude that poured from my eyes.

The mid-summer sky was beautifully clear. The morning breeze was gentle and cool. The white curtains waved quietly over the window.

Please grow up to be a beautiful and wise woman, I prayed, and selecting the *kanji* characters meaning "beautiful" and "wise," I named her Michiko.

Examples of Mrs. Nakamura's
calligraphy

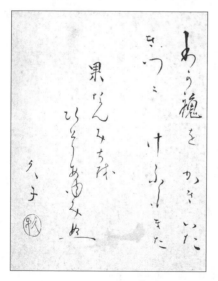

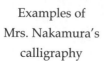

Examples of
Mrs. Nakamura's
calligraphy

Embracing My Invalid Husband

DURING THE TWO YEARS AND EIGHT MONTHS that we toured the northern area of the Honshu main island, my husband did not so much as catch a cold. But he suddenly weakened one day, and the days he spent in bed increased.

The fact that Mr. and Mrs. Ikeno, the owners of the show in which I was performing, looked down on Nakatani and considered only me, the "artist," to be important, bothered me a great deal. Their way of offering even a bowl of rice gruel or a glass of milk to Nakatani was so disrespectful that I became angry.

But this is not a time to be misled by emotion, I told myself sternly. I must cope with my husband's illness as best as I can.

Restoring my husband to health was the most important thing. But what would happen to my husband, to me, and to our child Michiko, if I remained here, I wondered. I considered all the possibilities for several days and nights, and finally concluded that we had to leave the Ikeno's group, even if we had to beg.

In April of 1923, after the show closed at the Sakurayama Entertainment Center in Morioka City, I requested permission to leave the Ikeno's group. Without taking time to even take a deep breath, we took a train to my husband's older brother's home in Kiryu City.

My husband and I had a simple banner made to advertise my act. Deciding to rely only upon ourselves, we went to Yokohama on July 1st. Just as we set foot in our new house, however, my husband staggered and fell, and was never able to rise again.

I asked the doctors at the Public Hospital, but none would tell me what my husband's illness was. Finally, I asked the head of the Negishi Clinic to make a diagnosis. He said that my husband had intestinal tuberculosis, and his condition had passed the point where anything could be done. Words failed me when I heard this.

For Michiko's sake, I wished to extend her father's life for even one day. I must not let her fall into the same situation as I, without a father, I thought, and cried and cried, but to no avail.

I asked for my husband to be hospitalized, but the doctor said, "You will just waste your money. It would be better if you let him rest at home, and give him whatever he wants."

On an afternoon in August, 20 days after the start of the month, when the summer winds blew morning and evening, I received a telegram from my step-father:

GRANDMOTHER SERIOUSLY ILL.
COME IMMEDIATELY.

I had been unable to be with my mother when she passed away, so I wanted to at least see my grandmother, whom I owed so much, one more time before she passed away. But how could I leave my seriously-ill husband?

My heart was distracted in a thousand ways. "Don't worry about me or our home. I'll get well if I just rest like this, so go and see your grandmother!"

Because my husband repeatedly said things like this, I finally asked my husband's brother and mother to take care of things while I visited my grandmother. I paid their travel expenses, the rent, and food. On the morning of August 27, I left Yokohama with both Michiko and a hired woman. My heart was torn between Yokohama and Takayama all the while.

Travel between Gifu and Takayama was possible only by bus then. I was told that in order to purchase two regular seats, reservations had to be made at least a week in advance. The only way we could get on immediately was to pay for reserved seats that cost more than 45 yen, which was a great deal of money at that time. After traveling all day, we finally arrived in Takayama about midnight.

Grandmother was paralyzed on one side, and further, could not even open her mouth. She just looked at me, tears pouring down her face.

My relatives were even colder than I had expected.

"Our home is not a *ryokan* (Japanese style inn), so please find a place to stay. If you don't make reservations quickly, you won't be able to get a room."

Were these the words from a person who shared the same flesh and blood as I? I was so sad, I could not reply. I no longer had anyone on whom I could rely ... no one to whom I could cling to and cry... It was natural that everyone was so cold, I told myself repeatedly; but still, I could not hold back my tears. After all the trouble of returning, I felt the least I could do was to have *sutras* chanted for my father, mother, and brother. But how I wished the fire of anger burning within me towards my cold relatives would die down, even if only while I was at our family temple and having the memorial service performed...

Hisako in her late 30s.

All Alone

THAT FRIGHTENING KANTO EARTHQUAKE hit the Tokyo area on September 1st, 1923.

All telegraphic communications were halted, which made me anxious about my husband's safety. When I learned that travel was possible between Chuo-sen and Shinsetsu-sen, I decided to return to Kiryu City. But because of my handicapped body and having to carry an infant, the woman I hired in Yokohama suffered from exhaustion and was of no further help to me.

I considered the problems that would arise from transferring to a local train and I asked my Uncle Umehata for help.

"I will see you as far as Kiryu," he replied, "but whether your husband is dead or alive, I cannot help you any further. If this condition is acceptable with you, I will accompany you."

These were the cold words of my uncle, whom I had contacted through my cousin, the night before our departure.

Tears were running down my cheeks when I replied,

"Whether he is well, or even if he is dead, I will never again come with my daughter seeking help in Takayama City!"

We reached Kiryu the fourth day after leaving Takayama City, September 8th, past 3 o'clock in the afternoon. My uncle took care of my baggage as soon as we arrived, and then left without so much as properly greeting my husband's family.

Even without feet, I practically jumped with joy that evening when my husband's older brother told me that my husband was alive and living in the Yakeno area. How grateful I was!

How could I complain about how cold-heartedly others treated me, as long as my husband was alive? I was so happy, the hardness that developed in my heart during the several days I was in my birthplace, felt as if a warm light was softening it.

Was my husband really still alive? The area had changed greatly because of the fires in the aftermath of the earthquake. Relying upon signs written on scraps of wood, we finally made our way to Yakeno.

My husband was alive! I clung to his chest and cried and cried. Although it could not have been helped, I still regretted leaving my seriously-ill husband behind to return to my birthplace. How deeply I regretted making my husband, who by then could not move freely, suffer in that disaster.

If for no other reason than to show how sorry I was for

having left him, I determined to do all I could to nurse my husband back to health. That was the least I could do as his wife.

Our house had not caught on fire, but the storm doors, *shoji* screens, wicker trunk, and even our night clothes and charcoal used for fuel; all had been stolen. Our home was just an empty house.

My husband's condition worsened every day. He got so that he did not even recognize me. "Who are you?" he would ask with a scowl. "Where are you from?"

But he never forgot our child. "Michiko! Where is Michiko? Quick, bring her to me...!" he would implore incessantly. He was by then almost unaware of his surroundings.

A hole about two and a half inches developed on the left side of my husband's abdomen and almost everything he ate flowed out of that hole. He was completely unaware of the discharge of his urine and feces, and this created even more difficulties. I could only ask others to do their best in cleaning up after him.

His appetite, on the other hand, remained excellent, and that led me to fruitlessly believe that he would somehow recover.

A memory I will always cherish is feeding my husband and daughter rice cakes containing milk, *kinako* (soybean flour), and *azuki* (red beans).

I planned to take my husband to his hometown when the weather became cooler and the trains began running regularly, and place him in a hospital where he would receive professional care. How I wanted to extend his life, for even one more day, as our daughter's father!

GRANDMOTHER DIED

This is the telegram I received from my step-father. My precious, darling *baba-sama* (grandmother) was no longer in this world. Although it was expected, still, how sad it made me. After a lifetime of toil, when her children should have been taking care for her; instead for the long period of 20 years, she was mother's right hand in raising me — my baba-sama. I was never treated like a deformed child while I was in my grandmother's care. Rather, I was treated like a guest. She taught me etiquette, how to eat, and many other things; but more importantly, she treated me like an ordinary child.

My grandmother taught me about Japanese sentiment through the collection called *Hyakunen Isshu*, "A Hundred Poems", and through the strips of paper on which the poems were written and then hung on bamboo branches during the Summer Festival.

During the Girls' Festival period, she sewed small wrapping clothes, called *fukasa*, for me so I could give them to my friends. When I cried in vexation because I couldn't do things the way I wanted, she would soothe and humor me while reciting the Nembutsu. That was how she raised me... my baba-sama, who was like the spring sun to me.

I had gotten in fights frequently and when I would inevitably be abused and taunted with, "Hand-less!" and "Foot-less!" and cry in vexation, my grandmother would always admonish me, saying, "The Buddha is watching, so you mustn't say bad things about others, even if you are teased and treated badly, and even if you are struck."

But after several days, even when I realized it was wrong, I would again get into a fight with others, and cause my grandmother to wring her hands in despair.

On my tours with freak shows, a *mawata* jacket and my favorite *arare* rice crackers in winter, and *mishima* beans in summer always accompanied me. Only my grandmother sent me these things.

Years later, I learned that she even set a *kagezen*, a meal regularly fixed for an absent person, for me.

Although I went to all that trouble to see her, she was unable to say even one word to me because of her stroke. And I was even unable to be with her during her last moments. I suppose that the Great Kanto Earthquake prevented me from being with her just before her death, but parting with her like that continues to be a matter of great sorrow for me.

Please, *baba-sama*, please forgive my unfilial behavior. *Namu Baba-sama.*

❊

Several days later, on a September day in 1923, just before dawn, my husband passed away at the early age of 30, leaving a wife without hands and feet, and a daughter just 13 months old.

I wanted to die with my husband. The pathetic pleas of the wife, "Live forever for the sake of your daughter," suddenly became futile. Holding our daughter in my short stumps of arms, I clung to the now cold body of my husband, unable to stop crying.

Not understanding what was happening, our daughter laughed innocently.

Although knowing how wide the division is between heaven and earth, I still could not help but reflect on the emptiness, the solitude, and the transiency of life.

Paper craft around Hisako's neck

Like the Mist

THE MORNINGS AND EVENINGS turned cold when the month of October rolled around. Although 17 days had passed since my husband's death, I did not make any effort to continue with my life. The days and nights in which I felt my heart removed from my body continued.

I had pawned most of my clothes so we could return to Takayama. Michiko's few clothes that we had left in our home had been stolen, so all we had to wear was a piece of old flannel clothing that the government had distributed to disaster victims. I had a little more than 10 yen in my wallet. My daughter and I were like tiny flames flickering in the wind, in danger of being blown out at any moment.

"You and your child are flesh and blood. Regardless of how you try, you cannot continue touring in a show carrying that child with your handicapped body. Who will look after you if something happens? What do you think will happen to your daughter then? You must think about the future."

"I know what sort of man Yuta Shinshi is. You and your daughter can rely upon him completely. I am sure everyone, including my dead brother, will rejoice for you from the Pure Land. Please do this..."

These words from the heart of my late husband's older brother, on my return to Shinshu, tired me in both body and heart.

I had wanted to wait at least until the 100th-day memorial service for my late husband before I decided anything. But the demands of eating today were so urgent, that Michiko and I did not have the luxury of relaxing for that long. If I were to remarry, the burden on everyone around me would become lighter.

That would mean falling into the same rut my mother had fallen into, I thought, but I had become a mother myself. In order to carry out my obligations as a mother, I had to overcome all difficulties.

Shinshi was born in Izu and raised in the downtown area of Tokyo. He was an open-hearted person. His family was in the dyed-goods business, but he was attracted to the entertainment industry when he was young, and so he became a student to a teacher of *naniwabushi* (folk storytelling). When not busy working, he would frequently be asked to participate on the stage. He did not drink, but could fit in anywhere in the entertainment industry. But what attracted me most about him was his fondness for children.

When our troupe was invited to entertain at banquets

or dinner parties, he would be surrounded by beautiful geisha and everyone would sing and dance riotously. Although the others frequently spent the night there, he would conscientiously return home to me in the middle of the night.

"Your body is not normal," he said honestly, "and I am, after all, a man, so I cannot promise I will never go out with other troupe members seeking entertainment, but I promise never to do so in a way that will cause you to suffer. I may make it difficult for you regarding household matters, but I promise not to cause you any problems because of drinking and being with other women."

A husband who can be relied upon — this is the greatest happiness for a woman.

After barely escaping from suffering and sorrow that almost stopped me from breathing, I felt the faint scent of femininity finally beginning to be released again.

I was to work in Yokohama, so we rented a small house in the city. That was where Tomiko was born.

"We must settle down in order to raise two children properly," my new husband said. "We should have a respectable home in Yokohama by the time Michiko is ready for school. You must leave the entertainment industry by then, and I will find work in a dyed-goods shop. Find some kind of work that you can do at home, and become a mother to our children, *ne*? So let's put up with this life for just a little longer and save the money to accomplish this."

Hearing my new husband's words, I was led to believe that even I could live a normal woman's life.

We had difficulties, but ours was a family life with a husband, wife, and children. If only we could have continued in that way; how much happier our two children would have been, both materially and spiritually.

This is a severe world in which we never know what will happen next, and it is impossible to know to what extent heaven will test us.

I will never forget: After performing at Boss Yamamoto's show on October 23rd, a memorial service for the war dead at Narashini, we had returned to Funabashi late that night. My husband, who had until then never requested anything special, said, "I'd like some sukiyaki, but I guess all the shops are closed …"

"Could you wait until tomorrow morning?" I asked. "I'll cook it for you, then."

Our young assistant went to bed soon after, and so did we. Not long after, my eyes were opened by the sound of my husband's moaning. I looked at his arms and legs. They were stiff.

I shouted at my husband, but he did not answer. The image of my late father's illness crossed my mind. I got up with a start and had our assistant run and get Boss Yamamoto.

"He has meningitis. There is no hope for a complete recovery."

That was what I was told at 2:00 am. Before morning,

three doctors had examined my husband, and they all said the same thing. I could not believe the disease had attacked my husband so quickly.

Please let it be a nightmare, I kept praying, but when dawn broke, my husband was still moaning.

On October 24th, 1925, at 3:00 p.m., the light of my husband's life was blown out at the early age of 35.

"Don't sleep, daddy. Take Michiko for a ride on the street car, *ne*?" The innocence of the little girl who didn't know her father was dead … pulling on his arm in an effort to wake him … not knowing the face of her real father, having a step-father who raised her so gently and compassionately like his own child, had passed away. What an unfortunate child. My heart felt as if it was cut through with sadness.

I lay next to my husband's now cold body that night, but could not sleep. I spent the entire night crying. The next morning, when I realized my husband was no longer with us, I did not have the will to get out of bed. How could I raise our two children alone? Why was only I left alive? I will live without relying on anyone!

I had blood relatives, but for me, they no longer existed.

How keenly I felt that those who are left behind suffer much more than those who leave this world.

My heart became even darker when our young assistant, who my husband had looked after so kindly, took advantage of the confusion and ran away with all of my husband's clothes, even his shoes.

74

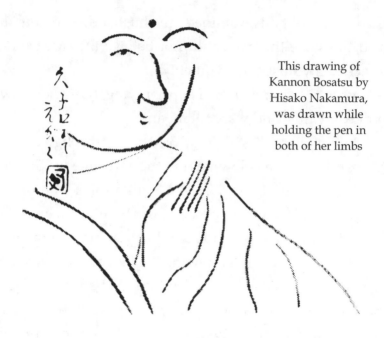

This drawing of Kannon Bosatsu by Hisako Nakamura, was drawn while holding the pen in both of her limbs

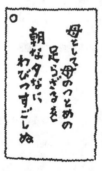

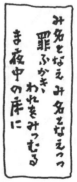

Calligraphy by
Mrs. Nakamura

A Woman's Heart

SITTING IN FRONT OF THE *BUTSUDAN*, the Buddhist altar, with the *sukiyaki* meal that I could not serve my husband the night before his death — what a strange *osonaemono* (offering). I closed my eyes and through tears, vowed, "I will raise our two children to be splendid adults. Please lend this weak person your strength so I can accomplish this..."

There being no other way for me to make a living, I returned to performing in Boss Yamamoto's show.

The cold December winds kept attendance low, so Boss Yamamoto requested a booking for me from the Tokyo temporary office. As a result, we left home in the Funabashi area of Yokohama where we had such warm memories, and went to live in Tokyo.

Tokyo is not a place where a peaceful and serene life can easily be led. My personal expenses were much greater when I worked through a booking office, and my savings dwindled. For this reason, I decided to tour the rural areas, taking my two children with me. It was not what I wanted, especially for my children, but there was no other way for me to survive.

What was most important in order for me to tour the rural area, of course, was a male attendant who would care for and make arrangements for me. The young man assigned to me by the Tokyo office, Sakaki, took care of everything. He worked hard on my behalf. Unfortunately for him, his wife had just passed away, leaving him with two children.

He was educated and accomplished in *ikebana*, the art of flower arrangement. He had a photography studio in the Tokyo area before the Great Kanto Earthquake, and at first glance, he was a most handsome man.

My sympathies for Sakaki gradually turned into love, and later, with Mr. Higashiyama as our *nakodo*, go-between, we became husband and wife. He was then 32 years of age, two years older than I. He liked to drink, and of course, like all men in the business, he liked to gamble. And because problems with other women occurred frequently, he was not a very good husband.

APRIL 26, 1927

On a broiling hot day in Taichu City in Taiwan, after an easy pregnancy, I gave birth to another daughter.

Although I was without a registered domicile, I decided to give this child the name Taeko, meaning "a wonder child." The show was closed then, and for a change, my pleasure-seeking husband was at home the day Taeko was born. However, he went out the third day after I gave birth and did not return. It was all the more trying for me because I knew just where he was, and even the woman he was with.

On a cold day in February of 1928, that reminded me of the bone-chilling place of my birth in Takayama, Taeko became feverish while I was performing in Miyako-no-jo City in Kyushu. Her entire body erupted in a rash, showing the symptoms of measles. But the rash disappeared completely one morning before the measles had run its normal course. Thinking this most unusual, I called a doctor. For some reason, the doctor took a long time finding our place. The time for me to perform was approaching, but the doctor still had not arrived. I asked an assistant to look after things, and entered the show hall, which was immediately in front of where we were living.

Whether good or bad, the hall was filled with customers. I cried in my heart at being in a profession that would not allow me to nurse my own child.

The young assistant did not say a word when he came to return me to our lodging, and I felt an ill omen. Taeko had stopped breathing. That was when the doctor finally made his appearance.

"Taeko-chan, why did you have to die? Please, forgive me Taeko-chan. Please, open your eyes just once more..."

I pressed my face against her still warm cherry blossom-colored baby cheeks, and wept without restraint.

The spring of next year, when our group was performing on the island of Shikoku, I placed Taeko's ashes at Zentsu Temple. But does this child, who gave the light of direction to a mother's heart, sleep there in peace?

May she rest serenely for eternity.

Calligraphy by Mrs. Nakamura

Performance Before the Emperor in Borrowed Clothes

ON A BRIGHT AUTUMN DAY in 1930 when chrysanthemums were in bloom, an *undo-kai* (sports day) was held at
the Gakushuin or Peers School for the children of nobility.
The Emperor of Japan attended. I was invited to perform
my poor act on that occasion.

It came about in the following way.

A man well-known in the Sanin district, named Takeuchi,
followed our act. He had exchanged *sake* cups with my
husband, which in the *yakuza* world is a pledge of inti-
mate ties between the two. Takeuchi's close friend from
college days was a man named Sato, who was as straight-
forward and open-hearted as a bamboo branch. Mr. Sato
was a teacher at the Peers School.

Because of Mr. Sato's recommendation, I was allowed
to bathe in the light of an unprecedented honor.

That day, Sato-sensei, my husband, and I went to the
Gakushuin School in a car sent from the Imperial Household Agency.

We were escorted to the lecture hall, where I was shown
a seat and asked to wait. After Sato-sensei's introduction,

I stood on the platform to speak. Or, at least I was placed on the platform. But Sato-sensei was a man who detested formality and ceremony, so with no indication of what he was about to do, he placed me on the table with the chrysanthemum crest of the Imperial Family, and proceeded to remove my artificial legs right in front of the Emperor and all the students.

Everyone was so surprised — they collectively drew in their breath in amazement. I was so embarrassed that I wanted to be swallowed up in the cracks of the wall. It would have been tolerable if Sato-sensei had discreetly removed my artificial limbs in a corner somewhere, and then placed me on the table, but he removed them right in front of the Emperor.

I cannot express how embarrassed I was, not only because I am a woman, but even more because it was done so openly before the Emperor. At that time, of course, everyone in Japan was required to worship the Emperor as a "living god."

Just thinking about it still makes my face turn red, and I break out in a cold sweat.

For my "act," I knitted, sewed, and made things out of paper by folding them (called *kamisaiku*), and ended up by brushing a poem on a long strip of paper called a *tanzaku*, with my mouth.

His Eminence, Mikasa-no-Miya, a lord-in-waiting, told me, "His Eminence the Emperor requests for you to brush another tanzaku."

I brushed a well-known poem by the grandfather of
the Emperor, Emperor Meiji:

Sashinoboru asahi no gotoku sawayaka ni,
Motama hoshiki wa kokoro naikeri.

Like the soaring
Morning sun,
Is how I wish
My heart to be

This tanzaku was presented to the Emperor. I was honored to see the Emperor carefully examine my poor calligraphy, and even today, I feel deep emotion when I recall
that moment.

Today, everyone can wear whatever they wish, but
back then, the clothes in which people appeared before
the Emperor were strictly regulated. I had asked Sato-sensei for instructions on the sort of clothes I should wear. He
suggested a garment with my family crest dyed upon it.
I did not, however, even have a change of clothing at that
time, let alone a garment with my family's crest.

With a friend as a guarantor, I rented a magnificent kimono in the Edo-zuma style with a one-piece obi sash. I
was dressed as I had never been dressed before in my life.
The cost of renting this costume for just half a day was
more than 15 yen, which was a considerable sum in those
days. I did not have that amount, so I ended up pawning
some things in order to raise the money.

I am probably the only person in all of Japan to

present herself to the Emperor in rented clothes. I was both ashamed and also filled with a deep sense of unworthiness.

The certificate of appreciation that I received from the Gakushuin School Hojin Association through Sato-sensei is a souvenir of this glory, during the first half of my life, and this honor is something I have carefully preserved.

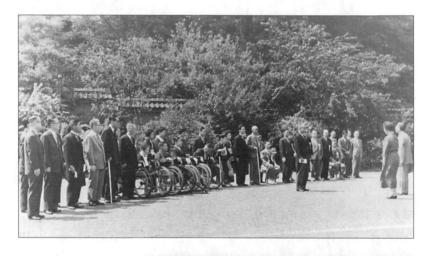

Hisako (in a wheel chair, far left) visits with Japan's Emperor Showa and the Empress, representing the disabled.

A New Husband

SAKAKI'S FAST LIFE AND LOOSE CONDUCT did not change at all, and so during the fall of 1933, with Mr. Ono of Kyushu as *chukai* (mediator), we separated.

Sympathy could have turned into love, but there was also the fact that Sakaki would always have a meal ticket with me around. When I further consider the situation, I don't blame him. Who would want to spend the rest of his life with a woman with neither hands nor feet?

Regardless of how emotionally involved we become, the side that wishes to separate is at fault. Perhaps it was a little belated, but this conclusion came into my heart from somewhere.

Although Sakaki took much condolence money for severing our marriage, he followed me wherever the show went and spread such malicious gossip about me, the entire group could not be booked anywhere. I began to feel I could not breathe because of not having a means of making a livelihood.

I was finally booked to perform in Hiroshima City, Kure City, and other places. And I was again troubled because of not having a male on whom I could rely. Again, through the good agency of Mr. Ono, I married my present husband, Toshio Nakamura, who was born in Shimane Prefecture.

Nakamura is nine years younger than I. He does not drink, and has a very modest and reserved personality.

When we married, Mr. Ono said, "It can't be helped if you two are separated by death, but please try not to separate while you are still alive."

I remember his words as if he spoke them yesterday. Although I am handicapped and cannot live without the assistance of a male, the fact that I married as many times as I did, must be considered shameful for a woman.

Toshio Nakamura married Hisako at 37, and took care of Hisako until her passing.

Regardless of how I try,
I am unable to live
solely through my own efforts.

I am allowed to live
while being unable
to do anything worthwhile.

With anger,
with sorrow,
without giving anything in return,
I am allowed to live this moment
without hands and feet.

I look into the mirror of truth
and peek through the window
of my mind...

What a dirty and frightening sight!
And even today,
this body without hands or feet
is allowed to live
in the limitless universe...

Ah, let those with spirit
find joy and happiness in this world.
That is my sole desire...

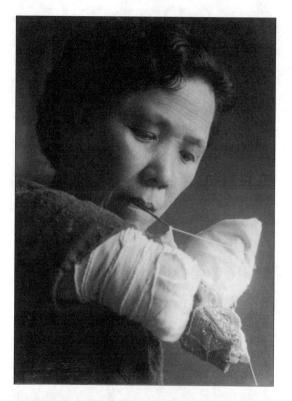

Top: crocheting with gauze wrapped limbs
and cutting thread with scissors

Light of My Heart

THE LATTER HALF of April, 1934...

One day, during the entertainment portion of the Rennyo Shonin Memorial Services, held at the west side of Mikawa, I became aware of a very refined-looking woman. She was wearing a beige *hifu* (a lady's coat worn over a kimono); at first glance, she looked like a nun.

She observed my performance through tears. She almost stumbled as she made her way to the exit with tears still running down her face. This made an impression on me that I cannot begin to express.

Our show was closed the next day because of rain. The refined-looking woman that I had noticed the day before inquired about me through an intermediary.

She was not a nun, but the wife of the late Shoshin Ito, Professor of Shinshu Senmon Gakko (Shinshu Institute), founder of the *Muga-ai* (love-without-attachment) movement, and a Buddhist lecturer and advocate.

Mrs. Asako Ito did not have hair on her head from childhood, which is considered to be a Japanese woman's very life. She was born into a family of physicians, but they could do nothing about growing hair on her head. During her youth, saying she had no need for long sleeves nor for a red obi sash, she made her way through life by wearing only a cheap obi made from coarse black cloth, and clothes in solid colors without decorations.

She did not continue on to the higher grades of school because she was so shy, and so, unknown to anyone, she spent her days in agony. Although she was born into a Jodo Shinshu family, she first had sought solace in the teachings of Christianity. She later received instruction from Ito-sensei and found what she was seeking in the teachings left by Shinran Shonin. They got to know each other through this contact, and later decided to marry. They were a well-known couple.

I was wondering how I could lead a more maternal life with my children about that time. And as my children grew older, that desire became even stronger. My desire to leave the freak show became so strong; finally, without first informing my husband's family, we went to Tokyo with my two children.

Asako Ito knew I did not have anything in the way of material goods, and felt that I might become destitute. She therefore organized a Supporter's Organization for me in Tokyo. I met many people during this time whom I will never forget. They include Chiba Kodo and Kan Kenso, who acted as Mrs. Ito's representative; supporters, such as Beiho Takashima; Doyu Izumi; Mr. and Mrs. Gilbert Bowles, who returned to Hawaii during the Pacific War;

Mrs. Raito Hirazuka; Mrs. Azuma Moriya; the publisher Kakuya Kurita; and many others.

Through the Supporter's Association, I was invited to many organizations in Tokyo, such as schools, *Fujinkai* (Woman's Organization), Mother's Association, Gathering of the Devout, and others, where I spoke of my experiences.

Deep in my heart, however, I felt embarrassed and began feeling unworthy as the center of attention in the organization. Regardless of how outstanding the people in the Supporter's Association were, if the person around whom the association was formed was not modest and humble, there was no meaning to that organization.

For myself, my purpose was not just to gather the one yen membership dues, per person, per month. I wanted some kind of fixed job where I could perform, and requested to be given such a position. This was during a time when there was no such thing as laws for the protection and benefit of the disabled. I could not appeal to companies for work because they could turn me down without reason. Spiritually and economically, I was stuck.

My husband asked a friend in Chiba City to act as his guarantor, and worked at things like delivering coal and working in a transportation company, but earning enough to feed a family of four was not a simple task.

That was when I studied how to make clothes for dolls, which until then was just a hobby, under a professional. I asked close friends and casual acquaintances to buy them,

and used the proceeds to help pay for my rent and to purchase food.

Since I had supported myself for such a long time, it was difficult for me to accept charity. To work and support ourselves—this is a difficult problem that constantly recurs in life—it is like the inevitable tide that flows up on a sandy beach and gradually forces itself on you.

When we were informed of the critical illness of my husband's father, we decided to return to Kokura City in Kyushu.

The Supporter's Association had dissolved by that time. In Kyushu, I again fell into the position of having to join a freak show, and felt like oil floating on water.

But in a life full of changes, the "Light of My Heart," that was given to me by Mrs. Asako Ito, did not go out, and this is a matter of great joy to me.

A jacket made for her
husband Mr. Nakamura
and a quilt for a bed.

A Woman of Light – Helen Keller

DURING APRIL OF 1937, HELEN KELLER, a great woman of darkness and silence, loved and admired not only in the world of the disabled but in the entire world, and known in Japan as the "saint of the three heavy sufferings" (blind, deaf, mute), came to Japan, the land of cherry blossoms.

I could identify with Miss Keller because I was blind for a while as a child.

Through the late Takeo Iwahashi, I had the good fortune to meet this wonderful woman. I wondered what sort of gift I could give this woman who could neither see nor hear. While thinking that my gift should be something that I made myself, I consulted with Reverend Chiba about what it should be.

"A doll would be a nice gift, don't you think?" Reverend Chiba asked.

I decided to give Helen Keller a Japanese doll, dressed in a beautiful Japanese kimono. I would, of course, sew the dress for the doll myself. I immediately began my task.

From the pittance received from pawning some things, I purchased a bit of cloth, and from part of the money I received from speaking engagements, I bought some gold brocade material to be used for an obi. The garment was not sewn particularly well, but I wanted to give something in which I had put my entire heart — to this person, from across the sea, who overcame the triple handicap of not being able to see, hear or speak-this sacred person of light.

With each stitch of the needle I held in my mouth, I felt we would truly understand each other because we were both handicapped. With a smile, I finished making the dress in the middle of the night of the 15th. Michiko dressed the doll with the garment I had made.

On the 16th, Reverend Chiba, the publishers of *Shufu-no-tomo* magazine, and I visited the Tokyo Daily News to publicize Helen Keller's appearance in Japan. On the 17th, I went to the Hibiya Community Hall with my teacher, clutching my doll tightly to my breast. On the table in the waiting room was a dazzlingly beautiful Japanese doll with a placard printed in gold letters, "Created by Takashimaya," the large department store. The doll had *tabi* (socks) made of white silk, and even had a *hakoseko* (decorative wallet) placed in its bosom.

Although each stitch in the kimono that I sewed was made with love and devotion, the kimono did not fit well because the doll was short and the sleeves were a little too long.

"Each stitch...was made with love and devotion."

My doll had a golden-sleeved undergarment, a crepe kimono, a purple and gold-embroidered obi sash with a
four-season floral design and a background of gold
chrysanthemums, and a small decorative rope over the
obi (which was made of material used by Michiko when
she was young). I added a white silk *obi-dome* (string
to hold the obi in place). Although I made the best doll
that I could, it had neither tabi nor hakoseko. Compared
with the doll presented by the Takashimaya Department
Store, my doll was very plain; a doll to be ashamed of.
Actually, that was the first time I had ever seen a doll with
tabi on its feet and a hakoseko in its bosom.

I should have asked someone who knew about dolls before making mine, I thought. But it was too late. "Sensei," I said, "let's return home. I'm ashamed to have my doll compared with that beautiful one. Let's leave."

"But we just arrived," Reverend Chiba said, "And you did bring your cute little doll. Let's wait a little longer."

The arrangements for this event were not only for Reverend Chiba or myself. Toshio Hirata, who was recommended by Iwahashi-sensei, put all his efforts into making Helen Keller's appearance in Japan a success. I could not arbitrarily leave on my own.

The appointed hour was fast approaching. The number of distinguished visitors increased. I felt as if there was not even a place for me to sit.

Mrs. Azuma Moriya arranged for me to meet Helen Keller, who was sitting on the dais. Suddenly a voice came from the dais, "Nakamura-san. Nakamura-san..." It was Iwahashi-sensei's voice. Assisted by Reverend Chiba and Mrs. Moriya's daughter, Yuriko, I went to the dais with my shabby doll.

Iwahashi-sensei introduced us. When Miss Keller's secretary/tutor, Ms. Thompson, translated his words to Miss Keller with her fingers, Miss Keller walked over to where I was sitting, and gave me a warm kiss. Then with her hands, she gently stroked both my shoulders. The moment she came in contact with the short stubs inside my sleeves, her facial expression changed. She then stroked the lower half of my body. When she real-

Hisako presented a doll to Helen Keller.

ized that both my legs were artificial, she again embraced me, and gave me another long kiss. Warm tears from her eyes, through which she could not see anything, wet my cheeks. I pressed my face against her left shoulder.

Not one of the more than 2,000 people in the audience raised a face—all that could be heard in the hall was the sniffle of tears. I was never so moved in my life.

Miss Keller held my shabby little doll on her lap and patted its head.

I shook with emotion when I saw her warmth.

When we work at something in which we put all our heart, there is neither ocean nor national boundary. The sacred and the true mind of human beings overcomes many obstacles in life—that is what I learned then.

Helen Keller came to Japan a second time, from August to October of 1948. I met her at the Kyoto School for the Blind during that visit. I was happy that she remembered me.

The third time we met was in June of 1961, while the leaves were still green. We met again at the Hibiya Community Hall.

It would have been a terrible waste if the few times that we had met ended in nothing more than a temporary deep emotion. I would like to believe I was able to at least glimpse into her gentle heart and mind, and had learned from it.

Hisako spoke to many
groups from this time on.

The Way of Reality

ONE EVENING DURING THE EARLY SPRING of 1938, I was invited to speak at a local *Fujinkai* (Buddhist Womens Association) in Tokyo. Among those present was a person who grasped a *juzu* (Buddhist beads) while gently reciting the Nembutsu. His name card read, "Worship in the morning, gratitude at night."

This was the calligraphy master, Kaho Fukunaga-sensei. Through him I had learned about Shinran Shonin, the founder of the Jodo Shinshu teaching.

The first book I read about Jodo Shinshu was *Tannisho Shinzui* (The Essence of 'Notes Lamenting Differences'), by Shudo Osuka-sensei. At a time when I had many problems and many anxieties filled my heart, I read the following words: "Recite the Nembutsu. Reciting it means leaving everything to the Buddha who, regardless of the circumstances, is always holding us sentient beings in his embrace. Please, say the Nembutsu."

For me, these words were like rain during a drought. I felt as if I was a tiny seed that had lain dormant in the ground for a long time, finally peeking above the ground for a glance around. I felt I heard the voice of my grandmother reciting the Nembutsu while holding me in her arms.

Regardless of how much I think about and try to solve problems by myself, what can I really do? I realized: Yes, that's it! I will recite the Nembutsu and leave it all to the workings of the Buddha! After all these years, I felt I was finally able to see the Way of Reality, narrow as it might have seemed at the time.

I lived the life of an "artist" in a freak show for many years. During that time, I had many chances to embrace religion. Whenever my wretched experiences in life would be described in a woman's magazine, I would receive many religious tracts, including copies of the *Old and New Testaments* of the Christian Bible, not only from within Japan, but also from foreign countries. I tried to read all the material sent to me.

And while I was living in Tokyo, Christians many times recommended that I be baptized.

I once received a book titled, *Seimei no Jisso* (The True Aspect of Life), written by a woman I knew very well. I read it, but there was nothing in it that shook my heart and mind. I wanted something deeper, more profound; something with the essence of life to it. I could not help but feel that somewhere, something existed that would truly satisfy me.

My place of residence was not fixed. Like a gypsy, I changed residences often, from Tokyo to Kyushu, from

Kyushu to Takayama, and back again; always moving from one place to another. But once the light of the
dharma began lighting up my heart, faint though it was,
it never went out—and for me—it was a source of great
happiness.

The teaching of Jodo Shinshu has deep roots in
Takayama. Buddhist services are held in that city year-
round. Takayama is a city where the voice of the Nembutsu never dies out, although I believe it may be a little
different now.

At any rate, for this reason, I was able to attend services
at the nearby *Betsuin* (a temple with a special relationship
with the Hongwanji headquarters in Kyoto) and temples
in the vicinity.

I wanted to hear more about the teaching that Shinran-
sama had left for us. Isn't there someone who can tell me
all I want to know, I kept wondering, and without realiz-
ing it, sought my *zenchishiki*, "a good and virtuous teacher
along the way."

As long as we are "allowed to live," we must continue
to live. In order to live a real life as a human, there is a
certain path to reality—the dharma—that I can pursue.

Then, I sought out books on Buddha-dharma, and
especially on the Jodo-Shinshu understanding of it. I
read books by Chion Matsubara, Joen Ashikaga, Shinryu
Umehara, Ryojin Soga, and Daiei Kaneko; all great
scholars with a great understanding of life and Buddha-
dharma. This was during World War II when books were

very difficult to acquire.

While living in my hometown, the person who watered the desert of my heart and mind, was my *tado tanka* (poetry) teacher, Jujo Fujiyama. He was also the *Rinban* (head minister), of the Takayama Buddhist Temple, and also administrator of the Takayama District of the Higashi Hongwanji organization.

Another person to whom I am deeply indebted is Senko Makino, of the Nishi Hongwanji organization, who twice a year, in the Spring and Fall, would come to Takayama on his preaching rounds.

Through the efforts of Mrs. Akiko Kato, I was allowed to spend a week on Ikuno Island in the Inland Sea where Reverend Ashikaga had a retreat, even though it was very inconvenient to travel.

The year after the war ended, I attended a seminar held at Reverend Akegarasu's place. I was also able to meet Reverend Umehara personally. By chance, I became rather close to the Professor and Reverend Shinsho Hanayama. He greeted me warmly whenever I went to Tokyo, and several times allowed me to stay at his home. I was able to receive his personal instruction, for which I will always be grateful. I believe the Jodo-Shinshu followers in the United States were very fortunate in having him as their *Socho* (Bishop) for as long as they did.

Leaving the Entertainment World

THE 1942 NEW YEAR'S SHOW OPENED in Tsu City in Mie Prefecture. That was the last show in which I participated. I left because the stump of my left leg and the stump of my right arm had been hurting since autumn of the year before.

I went to Tokyo near the end of January, when the cold winter winds seemed to blow right through me. I was examined by Dr. Kinoshita at the hospital associated with Nippon University. He decided to cut off about 3 centimeters from the limbs that bothered me.

February 27, 1942—a day difficult for me to forget.

My left leg and my right arm were operated on, as decided. Because of the shortages due to the war, however, a complete anesthesia was not allowed for the general public. All I received was a local anesthetic for the entire two hour and forty-five minute operation. I could see my flesh being cut and I could hear the bones being shaved off. The pain was so intense, greasy sweat poured from my face. But I did not let one word escape my lips about how much it hurt, or how much I was suffering.

That morning, Michiko gave birth to a baby boy in Numazu City. I prayed on my operating table for both mother and child to be safe and healthy.

In March, the *sakura* (cherry blossom) buds began turning pink. By the time I left the hospital, they were blooming. I stopped off at Numazu on my way home, and saw my first grandchild.

As a new grandmother, I thought, I should stop my gypsy-like existence. But I wanted to leave without making a scene. That was all I could think about.

I decided it would be best if I did not keep any of the items that are necessary to perform in a freak show, such as the *kesho maku* (curtain with my name on it that was draped over the platform on which I performed). So I sold everything. I was determined that regardless of the difficulties, I would never return to the world of freak shows.

My husband accepted a job in a nearby sawmill. Because of the war effort, Tomiko left school after graduating from the lower course and began learning to sew. She married after several years and began raising her own family.

I spent 22 years with one freak show after another. I traveled all over Japan and I also crossed the seas, performing in Korea, Taiwan, and Manchuria. During this time, I experienced everything humanly possible. I lived in the *yakuza* society, the world of gangs that controlled Japan's entertainment industry, with strict rules.

I lived with people in the entertainment industry,

where red blood seethes much more readily and also more violently than in general society. I also came in contact with many beautiful people, whose warmth and sincerity could not be exhausted, and which could not be bought with money.

Only because such a society existed was I accepted without prejudice for what I was, and allowed to live in my own way — even though I had neither hands nor feet. Although it was not very much, I was allowed to study and learn while I lived and worked in that environment, for which I am eternally grateful. It is absolutely not, however, a society that I can recommend to everyone.

Example of
Mrs. Nakamura's
calligraphy

Hisako taught herself to
do everyday activities.

The Daily Life of a Woman Without Hands or Feet

I AM FREQUENTLY ASKED how I go about daily life. The following may be of interest to those who wish to know how a physically handicapped person does things.

Toiletry–I open the container of tooth powder with my teeth. I grasp my toothbrush with both of my limbs and thus am able to freely brush both the insides and outsides of my teeth. I wash my face with both of my limbs. I wring out the towel by holding it in my mouth and with my limbs.

TAKING A BATH

This is something I am frequently asked about. If the bath tub is built high and deep, then I must have help to enter and exit; in the case of public baths, however, I can easily enter and exit by myself. I place the towel over my left limb and wash myself all over, including my face. To wash my back, I hold one end of the towel with my mouth, throw the other end over my back and hold it securely with my lower limb. Moving both my body and neck at the same time, I scrub my back.

GOING TO THE TOILET

If the toilet is inside the house, I can go by myself because, unlike Western toilets, Japanese toilets are built flush with the floor. If shoes must be worn, such as in public toilets, then I must have help. This makes it difficult when I travel.

CLEANING

Dusting–I place the duster under my right armpit and, with some support from my left limb, am able to use it to dust.

Sweeping–I place the broom under my right arm pit and sweep with a slight assist from my left limb.

Wiping Surfaces–Just as when I wash my face, I wring it out by holding it in my mouth and with both limbs. I wipe with my left limb.

Laundry–I pump the water and do all of the washing using my left limb.

COOKING AND EATING

I can't do anything that can be considered real cooking, but since I am a woman, a wife, and a mother, it is natural that I make a place for myself in the kitchen.

Rice–I rinse the rice with my left limb.

Kitchen Knife–I place the handle of the knife in my right armpit and use my left limb to press down to cut fish and vegetables.

Peeling Vegetables–I hold the tool in my mouth, hold the vegetable with my left limb, and peel.

Eating–I wrap bleached cotton cloth around my right limb, insert the *hashi* (chopsticks) within its folds, and balance the *chawan* (rice bowl) on top of my left limb. Incidentally, the cotton cloth wrapped around my right limb is extremely useful to me in many ways. For example, it serves as a very convenient pin cushion when I am sewing.

READING AND WRITING

Reading–I remove books from the shelf with my left limb and my mouth. I turn the pages of the book with my lips.

Using a Brush–When I brush small *kanji* and *kana* characters on material, such as *tanzaku* (long strip of paper on which to write poems), *shikishi* (long square poetry card), or *makigami* (rolled letter paper): I use my shorter right limb and my cheek to hold the brush. When I write characters that are a little larger, I hold the brush in my mouth. I rub the *sumi* block to create ink by using both my limbs.

Using a Pen or Pencil–When I write using an implement that requires pressing down hard, I hold it with both of my limbs. I am able to write postcards, letters, and manuscripts in this way. I can refill the ink in a pen by myself as well as sharpen a pencil.

SEWING

Cutting Material–I hold the scissors in my mouth and use my front teeth to open and close the scissors to make the cutting motion. I am able to cut materials such as textiles, cloth, and paper.

Marking the Pattern–I hold the ivory scoring tool securely in my mouth and mark the pattern.

Measuring Cloth–I place the ruler on my sewing table and then hold a marking pin in my mouth. Using both of my limbs, I hold the cloth against the ruler, and mark the dimension I want with the pin in my mouth. In this way, I am able to sew most things, such as *tanzen* (thickly-wadded large-size *kimono*), *kimono*, and *haori* (Japanese coat).

Cotton Wadding–When no one was around to help, my biggest problem was putting in the cotton wadding, but after much effort, I was finally able to do even this by myself.

Threading a Needle–I narrow the end of the thread with my lips. Next, I hold the needle in my mouth with the eye outside and the point inside my mouth. Holding the thread with both limbs, I then lower the eye of the needle over the thread.

Knotting a Thread- Using my tongue and lips, I make a loop at the end of the thread. Holding the thread with my teeth and lips, I pull on the thread with both limbs to create the knot.

Time Required to Sew- I can complete a *hachike* (type of *kimono*) or simple woman's dress in a day and a half to two days.

Ink for calligraphy

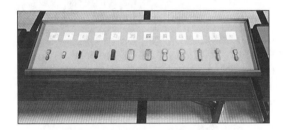

Hanko for signing calligraphy

Using a brush and hanko

Mrs. Nakamura with artificial limbs
standing with a friend.

Most people would complain that
they lack hands and feet.
The following poem expresses
Mrs. Nakamura gratitude,
saying she has everything she needs.

I Have Them, I Have Them All

A refreshing
Autumn morning. . .
"Please, hand me a towel."
A husband who answers, "Oi,"
A daughter who says, "Hai."

Brushing my teeth
And then removing my false teeth
to clean them further,
And washing my face. . .

Though short
And without fingers,
My round
And strong stump of an arm
Does everything for me.

A limb
Without a bone.
A soft arm,
A short hand.

I have them, I have them,
I have them all. . .
It's all I need.
What a refreshing
Autumn morning. . .

Hisako Nakamura expresses gratitude
saying she has everything she needs.

Great Indebtedness

THE JAPANESE EDUCATIONAL SYSTEM changed completely after World War II. As an uneducated person, I am unable to say whether this change was for the better or for the worse.

Regardless of the period of history, we Japanese were raised and enveloped in the love and compassion of both our parents. How can we ever forget our great indebtedness to them? I believe we have no value as human beings if our minds do not turn naturally in that direction.

"Knowing our *go-on* (indebtedness)" is what makes us human, and those of us who are allowed to recite the Nembutsu must be particularly aware of that.

After being saved from a dangerous situation, a fox, which in Japanese folklore epitomizes cunning, is supposed to have said, "Those who receive a favor but have no gratitude are just like human beings."

It is natural for a child to realize indebtedness to parents, but parents must not make their children feel the weight of that indebtedness. Parents should not assert their authority and thereby cause problems for their children.

"Listen carefully to what your children say." This is an ancient saying, and I believe it is the foundation for parents and children to get along together.

A parent's indebtedness to a child, and a child's indebtedness to its parents should be expressed in the form of attending temple and reciting the Nembutsu. But even if one attends temple, how can one understand Amida Buddha's Great Compassion without understanding the position of both parents and children? Otherwise there is no point in reciting the Nembutsu.

Especially now, Shinran Shonin's sacred teaching should be heard and held securely in our hearts. I hope we all look into the mirror of the dharma and follow the way shown by the Buddha. I am filled with gratitude for the limitless light of compassion that allows me to live strongly and fully today.

"Can I wear geta, too? I'd like to go outside, even if I have to toddle."

I hung the stumps of my legs over the side and cried and shouted—all while swinging the stumps back and forth. How I made my mother and grandmother suffer! I desperately desired to walk the great earth wearing bright red geta on my feet.

When twilight came, I wanted to go outside so badly, I almost couldn't stand it. Mother raised me on her back and took me outside, but she would soon say, "Uncle or Auntie will scold us if they learn about this, so let's return."

The moments I was able to grasp the beauty of nature in heaven and on earth, when I was able to sense its purity — these caused my childish heart to rebel against returning to that dark house. Being cooped up in a dark house, the resentment and sadness just grew larger and larger within my heart.

April arrived and school began and my dream of going to school with a group of classmates disappeared like a rainbow, never to return. Its disappearance was society's fault, or rather, was the fault of those who could have allowed me to attend.

A handicapped child who lived at home was not a credit to a family. A child without hands or feet made them feel humiliated; so they prevented that child from venturing outside and being seen by others. Thus, going to school was absolutely not allowed. I was firmly told that going to school and studying were not necessary for a handicapped person.

But, such an attitude by the average person is not just the attitude of the older generation. There is no difference — even today — in the treatment of those whom, through illness or through other causes, have become handicapped. They are considered to be a burden on society, and especially on their immediate family.

"You are very unfortunate not to have hands or feet,

"A deformed child doesn't need an education!"

The elementary school Hisako was not allowed to attend.

aren't you? It must be your karma from a previous life. You are repaying your karma from a previous life, so bear it as best you can."

"The fact that you do not have hands or feet must mean that a curse was placed on you, doesn't it?"

I heard statements like these from the time I became aware of things, and even today, until corns developed in my ears.

It is easy to dismiss such statements if they are from uneducated people who live in remote areas, but I have heard religious leaders and speakers with many degrees say to people with disabilities, "Your present situation is due to your karma from a previous life..."

I do not know what people of other religious denominations may say about this, but I believe such statements cannot be said by those who understand Shinran Shonin's teaching.

Because I am so unlearned, I am completely unaware

of the deeper and profound doctrines of the Jodo Shinshu teaching. How I wish those who urge disabled people to resign ourselves to their condition would first try to determine whether it is that easy. Unfortunately, the only way to do this is to cut off their hands and feet and let them experience being without those important appendages. Only then will they know just how much those of us without hands and feet suffer and sorrow.

I have spent 60 years living without hands and feet. I absolutely have not resigned myself to my fate.

The light of compassion that shines on the depths of my karma will not let me resign myself to my fate. The Nembutsu allows me to see this "self" for what it is.

The teaching of Buddha-dharma does not tell us just to make the best of what has happened, or to intellectually consider the causes and conditions that brought it about and put up with it the best we can. That sort of mistaken one-sided point of view is what has pervaded the thinking of the Japanese people and made Buddha-dharma a dead teaching. Saying "resign yourself…" is nothing more than covering up a bad odor, and serves no good purpose. Rather, it seems to me that not covering something, however disagreeable it may be, is far preferable.

Japan has approximately 400,000 disabled persons under 18 years of age. Not a single person in that group asked to be made disabled. Undoubtedly, their parents prayed for them to be healthy and happy.

I believe many physically and emotionally disabled persons existed in all past periods. That is all the more reason why the teaching of Mahayana Buddhism must be brought closer to us. I wish the teaching would spread even wider. Is this desire in vain?

Also, since this is not a matter of someone else's next life, nor the problems of another, I believe we must seek the true way more diligently. Follow a "good teacher," and listen to dharma.

A good mind arises, due to the influence of past good deeds; evil things are thought and done, due to the work of past evils. The late Master Shinran said, "Know that every evil act done — even as slight as a

NHK radio broadcast lecture series

particle on the tip of a strand of rabbit's fur or sheep's wool — has its cause in past karma."

As expressed in this passage from the *Tannisho*, because there is nothing that does not depend on "good karma," I would like to be able to recite the Nembutsu through the "good karma," that is the Great Compassion bestowed upon us by the Buddha.

I find it most sorrowful when parents who are considered to be followers of Jodo Shinshu, are so frequently engrossed in charms, spells, and prayers, that they do not seek proper medical treatment for their children with

 infantile paralysis, a cleft lip, or other birth defects.

I believe among the readers of this book, that at least a few may have a disabled child. I urge these people to forget about charms and spells, and seek proper medical treatment.

If, however, the body does not respond, then have the child use the part of the body that remains; the hands or feet, eyes or ears, which will allow that handicapped child to live fully within society. I believe such concern for a disabled child is the true compassionate heart of a parent.

The Nembutsu that you recite through the experience of having such a child will then be considered something that is "given" to you, and not something that you do through your own efforts. And the same time, you will be able to understand what a true resignation is.

Although the "parent" who allows me to transcend suffering and sorrow is here, I have forgotten my indebtedness to him, again today. What a sorrow!

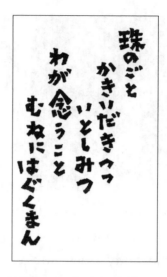

Calligraphy by Mrs. Nakamura

Hisako and her daughter, Tomoko to her right

Allowed to Live

IN THE DOCUMENT TITLED *Yokawa Hogo* (*Dharma Talk at Yokawa*) by Genshin, is the following passage: "… to be born a human being is a great joy! No matter how humble your station in life, it is not inferior to that of a *chikusho* (a being in the world of brute animals). Regardless of how poor your family, it is wealthier than a *gaki* (a being in the world of hungry ghosts)."

Before we disabled people lament that we do not have hands or feet, that we cannot see, that we cannot hear, or that we cannot speak; we should first rejoice for having been born human.

Regardless of our physical conditions, we are able to seek the way of reality because we were born human.

The most important gift that we have received as human beings, what each of us has without exception received, is our *kokoro*. This all-encompassing Japanese word means both our minds and hearts. No matter how much it is used, it never decreases. Regardless of how rough the storm, how steep the mountain path, the depths to which we fall in society, or are forced to endure days of poverty or a dark life of illness; what allows us to smile brightly and supports our physical body so solidly, — this is our kokoro.

More than 10 years had passed since the end of the Pacific War. Welfare laws have finally become a reality in Japan which is a great blessing in our time.

In the past, people looked upon us with cold eyes, making statements such as, "Those without complete limbs are not human." When I consider the great difference in attitude towards disabled people today, I cannot help but be grateful for our times.

But does that mean the hundreds of thousands of disabled persons who rely upon welfare for support are really "saved," either physically or mentally?

I believe that rather than receive financial support, disabled people should use the hand or foot, or eye or ear that remains, to support themselves as much as they can. Truly, that is the best way to live as a human being. To allow this, our politicians and the government must provide more places where those of us who are disabled can work.

I do not believe the hundreds of thousands of disabled people in Japan are concerned solely about receiving financial support. I wish more people who are important in society and the government would realize the majority of disabled people only wish for a place where they can be employed. We would like to live without having to rely upon others. Please, make such places available to us!

We disabled do not want to rely too heavily on our

society, or families, on our country or our government. Because we are allowed to live, rather than just exist, it is important that we strive and do the best we can. The teaching of the Buddha-dharma, regarding the past, is not just to make the best of what has happened; to intellectually consider the causes and conditions that brought it about and put up with it the best we can. We must use our best efforts to succeed.

It is most important now for us disabled people to open the "eyes of the heart." We must work together to become a beacon for our society, and show how to live bright and true lives.

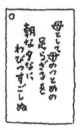
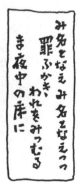

Calligraphy by
Mrs. Nakamura

Mother and daughter,
Tomoko

Handless and Footless

THAT GRIM AND GHASTLY PACIFIC WAR ENDED
on August 15, 1945. A year and two months after the
end of the war, my husband was repatriated from South
Korea, healthy and sound. I was grateful to the depths
of my being that he survived the war.

My daily needs were again taken care of by my husband and my daughter, Tomiko. Although we were very
poor, we renewed a bright and happy life. I began receiving invitations to speak, and the times when I had
to travel to different areas increased. At those times, Tomiko would use a *hoso-obi* (an undersash, a girdle used
by women) to hold me in place on her back, grasp a trunk
in both hands, and make her way through the post-war
throngs. After much effort, she was able to board the ve-
hicle that would take us to our destination. There were
no empty seats, of course, but many strangers kindly
gave up their seats for us.

"It must be difficult carrying such a large person on a
hot day… is she your mother?" people asked her. "That's
not an easy thing to do. I admire you…"

As if awakened from a dream, I was again taught how greatly I am indebted to my daughter when I heard words like these from strangers. Tomiko became my hands and feet wherever I was invited, from the extremes of the island of Shikoku to the greater Tokyo area. I could not help but realize how much I took her for granted.

Although I had decided not to accept Michiko's, (my other daughter) help after she married, I nevertheless continued to rely upon her, which I regret.

An unpleasant feeling arises within me when those who are curious about the mistress of a household who does not have hands and feet come unexpectedly to satisfy their curiosity. Among such curiosity seekers are those who believe I am somehow able to grant them benefits of some kind. Others think I am the founder of a religious cult. I often have a good laugh with the members of my family when such people leave.

The skirt I wear is so worn out that it is a skirt in name only. The stumps of my arms are always left uncovered, and when necessary, I cook rice and make one or two kinds of side dishes in the kitchen like everyone else. I serve my guests tea. Many seem to believe that because I do not have hands or feet, I have a different sort of consciousness, but in that regard, I am absolutely no different than anyone else.

Nothing is more frightening in this world than to feel that what we *itadaku* (received) has been taken for granted. Because I wished my daughters would be able to accept things with gratitude, I let Tomiko leave my side. She is presently living by herself.

Sometimes I receive compliments like, "You are a great person, but so is your husband."

Seeing those who come to hear me speak place their hands together in gassho towards my husband, I am again made to realize my great indebtedness to him for being my hands and feet.

Although I am very selfish and short-tempered, my husband takes very good care of me. Although I always forget to be grateful for his help and grumble about my dissatisfaction in this world, he never complains.

Traveling during the end of the year with the cold winter winds blowing through us, or during the middle of the year under the hot summer sun, is not easy. It would not be too bad if the trip was for only a few days, but when we are on the road for two, three weeks, or a month, it must be exhausting for him.

When there are no seats left in third-class, he places a discarded newspaper in the aisle and lets me sit on it. He stands next to me, making sure the passengers do not step on the stumps of my legs. It must be tiring to always be on the watch so no one steps on me.

During the short period we have to change trains, he carries our many pieces of luggage in both hands, hurrying in the underground passages with me on his back.

How sorry I feel for him when I see the greasy sweat

on his forehead and around his neck, and wonder how I can make it up to him. My husband performs the hardest sort of manual labor at such times. The sponsor who invites me to speak always comes to pick us up, and when he or she is considerate enough to wait for us at the station platform, I am so happy, I feel I have been reborn.

I am allowed to live in this way, through the great efforts of my husband and all those around me, even though I have neither hands nor feet.

The devoted Mr. Nakamura

Mr. Nakamura took Hisako to her lectures.

He was a generous man and always
recited the Nembutsu.

Calligraphy by
Mrs. Nakamura

The Unimpeded Path

SINCE THE FALL OF MY 20TH YEAR, for a period of 22 years, I performed in a freak show. I married into the business and became the mother of two daughters. During that time, I was separated from two husbands by death, another by divorce, and had major surgery for abdominal cancer.

I did not make much money as an "artist" in a freak show, of course; and there were times when I did not know where the next meal for my two daughters, or the *tabi* to put on their feet, would come from.

Why didn't I reach out for a helping hand or grasp for a voice of salvation while I was suffering in the depths of despair? Weren't there any of the religious cults that promised money, or promised to cure illnesses, remove difficulties, etc., in the mid-1920's?

Yes, many such cults exist in every generation. So many hands and voices invited me to join them, as I struggled in the depths of sorrow, that I became tired of refusing.

But what was it that would not allow me to join such cults?

I was 12 years old when my step-father borrowed money to expand his business. The building immediately in front was the Tenrikyo meeting place where my late father brought me to receive the blessings of that religion.

"If you discard the way, you will be discarded. Those are the kami's words, so please continue along the way." Mother was often told this by the Tenrikyo teacher. Although she did not seem to be a particularly devout follower, she attended the services from time to time. Since I was not invited to visit the homes of relatives or neighbors very often, the greater part of my time, until the fall of my 20th year when I joined the freak show, was spent at the Tenrikyo meeting place.

When I was 16 years old, the "meeting place" became the "place to spread the teaching," and I was asked to assist in the services. I learned to place a *hera* (spatula) in the bandages of my left arm stump and used it to play the koto. I also learned to read and sing the *kagura* (sacred Shinto songs). Although I did not have hands to actually do it myself, I was able to correct the hand movements of others when the teacher was away on missionary tours. For these reasons, I was called "Hisa-chan of the Tenrikyo teaching."

Although I did not have any formal education, through self-study I gradually learned everything from religious texts and books up to the sixth grade, which was then, the minimum required by law. I wanted to read everything I could, regardless of what was written on it. I never allowed a scrap of paper to pass in front of me without at least seeing what was written on it. Thus, although I could not understand them completely, I pored over all the books on the Tenrikyo religion maintained in the *Senkyo-sho*.

But as I grew older, the more I listened to the teacher's talks, the more I read the books, the more my heart felt alienated from the Tenrikyo teachings. I was not able to become a devout follower, who was able to bow my head to the Tenrikyo teaching.

This was because my late father often brought me to the Tenrikyo place in the middle of the night. He went into the chillingly-cold nights wearing straw sandals, unconcerned by the falling snow, and for two or three hours at a time pleaded for me to be cured by the Tenrikyo kami.

Over and over, while I was howling in pain from the cold, he would tell me gently, "*Kannin* (please forgive me). Daddy was wrong. I am trying to make it up to you now. Please, forgive me!"

His pleading voice remains with me even today. I wondered just what my father had to be forgiven for. Only after hearing from the Tenrikyo minister teacher what he told father regarding the disease in my limbs, did I finally understand my father's words. The Tenrikyo minister said my hands and feet were cut off because my father broke his promise to marry the girl he had loved.

Although my father was extremely dedicated to the Tenrikyo religion and had made many offerings to the

Tenrikyo kami that left him with a large debt, he died before he was 40 years of age, when he should have been in the prime of his life. He staked his life on praying to stop the pain in my four limbs, but after 14 years of pain, rather than becoming well, those limbs only became shorter. I cannot help but feel that, wherever he may be now, my father must regret his efforts. My poor, poor, father! How I sympathize with him.

"Regardless of how Hisa suffers, she will not give in. Please, rest assured, that even if she does not have hands or feet, she will live strongly and properly!" I do not know just when it was, but somewhere deep in my heart, this determination developed within me.

I believe it is most improper to use religion as a means to raise money, to avert calamities, or to cure illnesses. To substitute religious faith for medical science, and to consider religion a tool for gaining present-day benefits is, I believe, outrageous. The purpose of religion is to teach us how to live without injuring others, to teach us how to live strongly through all difficulties, regardless of the circumstances, regardless of our physical condition, for as long as we are alive.

Buddha Mind

I AM OFTEN INTRODUCED with well-intended words such as, "Today's speaker has neither hands nor feet, and undoubtedly has something very meaningful to impart to us."

For me, however, being held in anticipation like that is difficult to bear, and actually a source of sorrow.

The following passage from the *Tannisho (Notes Lamenting Differences)* moves me a great deal. Once a person traveled more than ten provinces to the capital city of Kyoto in order to ask how to be born in the Pure Land. The answer this person received was, "For me, Shinran, there is nothing left but to receive and believe the teaching of the Venerable Master that we are saved by Amida merely through reciting the Nembutsu."

What it means to me is, "I have no learning, and unlike you, I do not even have faith. I am only able to hear the Nembutsu as the greatest of treasures."

When I see faces staring at me while I speak, clearly saying, "I know that already! I don't need to be told that," it seems to me, the voice of the Jodo Shinshu Nembutsu teaching does not reverberate very deeply in their hearts. This may seem very disrespectful, but I cannot help but feel that way.

There are times, when the setting sun is about to drop below the mountain ridges, that I sit quietly by myself in the temple's study and close my eyes to examine my heart.

Long ago, from parental love and a desire to heal my illness, my father became a member of the Tenrikyo religion. But the kami of that religion allowed my father to leave this world at an early age, and did not heal either my hands or feet. Although I do not say that I bear a grudge against that religion, still, I do not have very good feelings towards it, either. That was my attitude towards the Tenrikyo religion, but one day it occurred to me to ask, "Did I really benefit from that religion?"

Yes, I did receive a great benefit. If the fervent prayers that my late father offered to the Tenrikyo god on my behalf more than 50 years ago had been effective, my arms and legs would be much longer than they are now. Not only that, I would not have had any of the pain or suffering. And if that had been the case, just what sort of mental state would I have lived with until today?

I would have considered it natural to make unreasonable requests of gods and buddhas when I suffered and sorrowed. And I would have considered religion to be something we embrace for some tangible physical benefit. If that was the case, then I probably would not have sought out the True Dharma. I would not have searched for the truth.

Although I did not receive any physical benefits, I received great spiritual benefits that cannot be seen with the eyes. I learned that earning more money than necessary to support yourself, averting calamity, curing illness, and other such desires are not what is truly important. This is what the Buddha has blessed me with.

The lack of effect that my late father's fervent prayers had were what caused me to seek the way of truth or reality. I believe they were an admonition for me to do so.

My father's mind, I cannot help but feel, was the great, wide, boundless "Buddha mind" itself.

Many *zenchishiki* (good and virtuous teachers along the way) have led me to where I am today. However, I now realize, unlike other people, my real *zenchishiki* was my body, — this body with neither hands nor feet.

I cannot help but feel it is my karma, my anguish, my suffering, my sorrow; all which have allowed me to recite the Nembutsu, and to transform difficulties into happiness and gratitude. This is the great gift that through the True Dharma, (through Shinran Shonin's teaching) I was allowed to hear from my many teachers, but it was my disabled body that allowed me to experience it.

The Mirror Image of Shinran Shonin.
Known as the *Kagami no Goei,*
(1173–1262), by Sen'amidabutsu

Example of
Mrs. Nakamura's calligraphy

Yearning for Shinran-sama

For the 14 years
After my hands and feet were amputated,
And I had fallen into the valley
Of suffering and poverty,
What intervened and supported the flickering light
That was my life,
And vowed that it must not be blown out,
Even during the typhoon-like days
And stormy nights,
Were my late father and mother…

The benefits we receive in this world are unlimited
When we recite Namu Amida Butsu.
The evils of constant transmigration are extinguished
And the evil karma of dying young is removed.
The person who taught me this was Shinran-sama.
It was you.

The suffering of being without hands or feet
Was made the great condition
That allowed this most evil of persons who I am,

To be assured of Birth
In the World of Greatest Joy
In this world that is now so bright with light,

Oh, how wonderful!
I am allowed to hear this teaching of
Buddha-dharma that is so real,
The person who gave me this ultimate happiness
Was Shinran-sama.
It was you.

This difficult to live life
That I am now allowed to live,
This difficult to come in contact with happiness
That I am now in contact,
This difficult to hear True Dharma
That Shinran-sama allowed me to hear...
Today, too, I am allowed to express my yearning
Within the Nembutsu.
Truly, truly,
I thank you

Fulfillment of the Compassionate Vow

SUNDAY, SEPTEMBER 5TH, 1964. It was a clear fall day. The day for the service to present the Hiba Kwannon Bosatsu finally arrived. The sculptor of the image is the Reverend Jokyo Mishima, minister of Shinren Temple in the city of Takayama (a temple affiliated with the Higashi Hongwanji School of Jodo Shinshu). This was the temple that ministered to the spiritual needs of generations of the Kamanari family, within which I was born.

The presentation was held in the compound of Kokubun Temple in the city of Takayama.

The *doshi* (leader of the service) was Roshi Mumon Yamada. He was the President of Hanazono University, and also Resident Minister of Hosan Temple in Nagai City in Yamagata Prefecture. Inouye Jyoshin-shi was the first to arrive. People gathered from all over Japan, from the Kanto area (greater Tokyo area), Chukoku area, Kansai area, and from around Tokai. All in all, more than 300 people gathered for the service.

Those who took the place of my hands and feet in making this service a reality included: Shinichiro

Iwamoto, Mayor of Takayama City; Densuke Kakimoto, head of the Takayama City Council; Kiyoshi Hirabayashi, President of the Japanese Association of the Disabled; Kiyosho Maki, President of the *Takayama City Minjiho* newspaper; Yoshie Tachibana, former City Councilman; and many others.

Kwanon Bosatsu Sculpture

When we call our mother

When we call our mother
With all our might,
The visage of a flower
Gently rises.

Ah, even the sorrow
Of living today
Is melted when
We cling to that hand.

Kwannon-sama
Who arouses such nostalgia
And in whom
We take such joy.
The Compassionate Mother
Kwannon Bosatsu.

When we call our mother,
Our hearts become damp
With the look of love.

Ah, the mist of suffering
In the world of humans

Is cleared up
In the desire for us
Of Kwannon-sama

Who awakens such nostalgia
And in whom we take such joy.
The Compassionate Mother
Kwannon Bosatsu.

How I sorrow

How I sorrow
And wonder about
The evils I committed
In the past
That I must worship
Without hands to place
In *gassho* today…

Late at night
Tears wet my cheeks
When I consider that
My present suffering
Is solely due to my past evils…

These two poems express Mrs. Nakamura's
understanding that she can live fully in the present
only by taking complete responsibility for her past.

Though Without Hands or Feet

Though without
Hands or feet,
The life that
Is allowed to live. . .
How precious.

Because I am without hands
And without feet,
I am enveloped
In the Buddha's
Compassionate sleeves!

How peaceful I am…
Though unable
To repress the wrath
In my heart,
The Buddha accepts me
Just as I am!
Namu Amida Butsu.
Namu Amida Butsu.

After a moment of irritability
I reflect,
And prostrate myself
In repentance before the Buddha.
What should I do
About my selfish desires?
I can only leave them in
The hands of the Buddha.

The white chrysanthemums
I offer the Buddha...
Its pure scent remains
As I chant the morning *sutra*.
The cheapest of rice gruel
allows me to live.

The worship
brings such happiness.
The karma which the mother bears
And the karma which she
Forces her daughters to bear...
Are all borne by the Buddha
So I must do my part
By living to the fullest today.

Sixty years
Without hands or feet
Only because the Buddha's
Compassionate hands and feet
Have taken the place of mine...

Mrs. Nakamura's personal items

Hisako Nakamura and Me

"I WAS DEEPLY IMPRESSED by the article, 'Look at This Elderly Woman,' in the April 20th issue of *Tokyo Zakki*. All Jodo Shinshu ministers in the United States should use this article as the basis for their next dharma talk."

Many followers of the Jodo Shinshu teachings are readers of the *Hokubei Mainichi* newspaper, so I am sure they will be very happy about an article like this. I heard many comments from Buddhist followers in this area.

I would like to know more about Mrs. Nakamura, who seems to be a *myokonin* (a person enlightened through the Jodo Shinshu teachings) because of her deep-seated faith. If she is at all competent to speak before groups, I would definitely recommend her to be invited to speak to Jodo Shinshu groups, such as the Fujinkai (Buddhist Women's Organization). If you know her address, I would like to make an offering to Mrs. Nakamura.

— A reader in Watsonville

The above is an anonymous letter printed in the *Hokubei Mainichi* newspaper.

I read more about Mrs. Nakamura in a column entitled 'Nippon Tayori' (Japan Diary), written by Mr. Shogo Muto, and published in the *Rafu Shimpo* Newspaper. I received many letters from people who said they wished to learn more about this woman.

The Buddhist Churches of America (BCA) had a practice which began prior to World War II, inviting a speaker from Japan every year to spread the dharma in the United States. I thought it would be a great consolation to the Japanese in the United States (who were then in a state of almost complete collapse from the defeat of their mother country in a world war), if they could hear this woman who had lost both of her hands and both of her feet at the young age of 2 years and 10 months. Even with her disabled body, she was able to cook, sew, and even write by holding a brush in her mouth. In the later years of her life, she encountered the teachings of Jodo Shinshu, and lived a complete life of the Nembutsu.

Accordingly, at the National *Fujinkai* Conference held the next year, I entered a proposal that the Fujinkai invite Mrs. Nakamura to the United States to speak to us. Unfortunately, that proposal was rejected.

Since I had to ascertain whether she would actually come to the United States before entering the proposal inviting her, I asked Mr. Tozo Yahata, Vice President of the West Los Angeles Buddhist Temple where I was then assigned as a minister, to visit Mrs. Nakamura at her home in Shizuoka City on his trip to Japan. This was a year before I entered the proposal.

After returning to the United States, Mr. Yahata reported, "Mrs. Nakamura has neither hands nor feet, but she has a far more sunny disposition than I, who have both. Her attitude put me to shame. She seemed extremely delighted about being asked to speak to us in the United States. . ." Unfortunately, as already mentioned, my proposal to invite her was rejected.

From a sense of personal responsibility (by being unable to carry out my end of the promise to invite her to the United States), I visited Mrs. Nakamura at her home in Shizuoka City when I visited Japan in 1965.

Attended by her husband, Mr. Toshio Nakamura, Mrs. Nakamura came all the way to the Shizuoka train station in a wheelchair to greet me.

I went to visit her in a mood of apology, but conversely, I was treated to a splendid meal, and further was loaded with gifts. And when it was time to leave, she went to the trouble of calling a photographer to record my visit. I will never forget the graciousness with which Mrs. Nakamura treated me in ways that I not only did not deserve, but in ways that were least expected.

That was the first time I was privileged to meet her, and unfortunately, was also my last parting from her. Mrs. Nakamura passed on to the Pure Land three years later.

I received an invitation to her funeral, but unfortunately, was unable to attend.

I thought that at the very least, I should pay respect to her grave. I was able to do so due to Mrs. Nakamura's second daughter's kindness, when I visited Japan again in 1980. My sole consolation was being allowed to chant a sutra before her grave.

Bunyu Fujimura
Former BCA Minister

Mr. Bunyu Fujimura and Hisako Nakamura

Letters Received from Mrs. Nakamura to Rev. Bunyu Fujimura

FIRST LETTER

Haisho, (Greetings).

Thank you for your letter of December 3. I am indeed honored to have your friendship.

I am much obliged for the visit by Mr. Tozo Yahata to my home on the 8th of December. Please give him my warmest regards...

At your request, I am sending 40 copies of my booklet, *Watashi no Koete Kita Michi* (*The Road I Traveled*). I hope you can find some use for them.

I gratefully await the opportunity of meeting you in your country next year. I am an uneducated woman but I hope I will live up to your expectations. The theme of religion is not very strong in my small works, and I am afraid they will not satisfy those with deep faith. I hope you understand that what little I have written is directed more to the schools, woman's organizations, and other groups that ask me to speak before them, and therefore are not religiously oriented.

I would appreciate knowing as soon as possible

approximately which month and day you wish me there. I have many requests to speak here in Japan, and I would like to plan ahead as much as possible...

SECOND LETTER

Akemashite omedeto gozai masu, (Happy New Year!)

Today, I received the letter you sent on the 30th of January.

Regarding religious booklets, have you been able to acquire the August and September 1957 issues of *Dobo* magazine, and July 1958 issue of *Daijo* magazine? The articles 'Kai Wariko-Sensei to no Taidan' (Conversations with Wariko Kai) and 'Nayami no Hate Ni' (The End of Agony) were printed in them. As you must know, these are just brief descriptions of my personal experiences and understanding.

As for radio broadcasts, I held one for the national radio station NHK 10 years ago, and also during the latter part of last November (for three nights), but these were mostly directed towards the disabled, and there is very little in them of a religious nature.

I became quite close to the Reverend Shinsho Hanayama, who was recently appointed Socho of the BCA. He will leave for the United States around April or May. I am sure you will learn a great deal from him.

I am very grateful that, according to your letter, you have written about me to those who are living in Hawai'i. Mr. and Mrs. Gilbert Pauls, who are in their 80's, live in

Hawai'i. They are very interested in Japanese culture, and lived in the Shibamata area of Tokyo until the middle of the war. He is a Christian minister, and long ago was a sponsor of my supporter's association (Koenkai), who treated me like his own child. How I miss him!

As you know, I have not received even *tokudo* (the first level of ordination). I am nothing more than a layperson, and therefore, I am not sure how helpful I will be in your efforts to propagate the Jodo Shinshu teachings in the United States.

I am carried by my husband to wherever I am invited to speak, and he is my sole means of conveyance. I speak at associations for the disabled and institutions associated with the Ministry of Justice (prisons, juvenile homes, etc.), schools, women's organizations in general, friendship associations, kindergartens, and similar places. Accordingly, I have not had the time nor the opportunity to write a book or even a pamphlet on my religious understanding…

THIRD LETTER

Haisho (greetings),

The rainy season is upon us here in Japan, and during the day, summer appears to have arrived.

I received the letter you sent on the 6th about five or six days ago, and today I received money and so many gifts that I am completely unworthy of receiving. I do not know how to thank you enough for them. (note: the gifts that Mrs. Nakamura received were from ministers such as Reverends Enjitsu Hojo and Gibun Kimura, and many devout members within the BCA who were moved by her.)

I read in the *Chugai Nippo* newspaper that Shinsho Hanayama-*Sensei* is about to leave for the United States. Please give him my warmest regards when you meet him.

I will put myself in your hands if the opportunity to visit your country arises again, but please do not be concerned about my being unable to visit the United States. I have decided to rewrite the latter part of the booklet, *Watakushi no Koete Kita Michi* and republish it, and to this end, I am taking up my pen every night.

Please take good care of yourself, and keep up the good work in spreading the precious teaching of Jodo-Shinshu. Thank you for everything you have done for me.

June 15th
Hisako Nakamura
P.S. My poor poem for the Reverend Bunyu Fujimura:

Sixty years
Without hands or feet,
Led by the compassionate hands
Of the Buddha. . .

FOURTH LETTER

Gassho,

I wish all happiness for your younger brother, who has now returned to the Pure Land. I read with tears of sadness, the news of his passing.

And I recalled the visit you paid to our home on December 28th of last year.

I would like to sincerely apologize for the long period during which I had not written. Please, forgive me.

Since the establishment of the Hiba Kwannon monument, the number of people asking where I live has increased so much, I have finally returned to my place of birth here in Takayama. I wanted to let you know my new address, but just kept putting it off, for which again, I ask for your forgiveness.

Although the snow piles up a foot and a half, my room is so well insulated that I do not feel the cold at all. I am very grateful for the comforts of this generation.

I received the 10 dollars you sent me from Mrs. Watari. I am extremely grateful for this thoughtfulness, and am unable to express my thanks enough. I made use of the return envelope you enclosed to express my thanks to Mrs. Watari.

The service for Kwannon-sama was held again this year, and we are presently making plans for the service next year. That we are able to do so, is due solely to your great help.

I wish for you and your wife to take good care of yourselves in this great cold.

Thank you for the *orei* (gift), and my condolences at the loss of your brother.

Sincerely,

While I am at it, please give my regards to Reverend Professor Shinsho Hanayama.

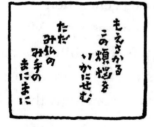

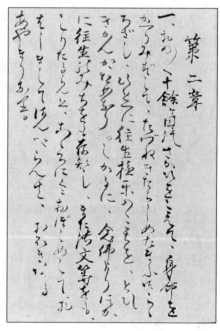

Example of
Mrs. Nakamura's
calligraphy

A Chronology of Hisako Nakamura's Life

November 25, 1897. The first child born to Eitaro Kanamari and his wife Aya in the city of Takayama in Gifu Prefecture.

1899, age 3, frostbite on her limbs developed into gangrene, ultimately resulting in the loss of her hands and feet.

Fall, 1901, age 5, younger brother Eizo was born. At age 7, her father died. During the fall of her 8th year, her mother remarried, and she became a member of the Fujita family.

1904, age 8, Hisako was not allowed to enter primary school. She began to learn by herself.

Spring 1906, younger brother Eizo, age 5, was placed in an orphanage, and just prior to his death, was the last they were to see of each other.

1907, age 11, strict disciplining by her mother and grand-mother began. Hisako made a kimono by herself for the first time.

November 6, 1916, age 20, left her home town of Takayama to become a member of a freak show. A month later, she worked in the city of Nagoya, billed as Daruma Musume (The Daruma Daughter). She performed all over Japan, Korea, Taiwan, and Manchuria.

1920, brother Eizo died in May and her mother died later that year in August. Her essay appeared in *Women* magazine, and won first prize. The same year she was given artificial legs.

1921, age 24, married Yuzo Nakatani. Their first daughter, Michiko, was born during August of the following year.

September 1923, age 27, separated from her grandmother and from her husband Yuzo by death. In November, married Yutaro Shinshi.

August 1924, second daughter Tomiko was born.

October 1925, husband Yutaro died. The following year married Toshio Sakaki.

April 1927, age 31, third daughter Taeko was born. Taeko died during February of the next year.

1930, performed knitting, sewing, calligraphy etc. for the Emperor of Japan.

August 1933, divorced Toshio Sakaki.

1934, age 37, last marriage to Toshio Nakamura.

1937, age 41, ended her life as a freak show "artist" and moved to Tokyo. Met the world-famous Helen Keller at Hibiya Community Hall in Tokyo, in April of that year, and presented her with a doll wearing a kimono she sewed with her mouth. She began receiving invitations to speak before different groups from that time on.

1938, age 42, encounted the *Tannisho*, which made her spirtually awakened. Introduced by Mr. Gaho Fukunaga, a calligrapher.

1940, age 44, returned to hometown and studied Buddhist books. Became the first president of the association of the disabled in Takayama. Began to speak before Fujinkai, Mother's Organization, Buddhist groups, at temples, disabled veteran's groups, schools, and prisons. Transported on the back of her husband or her daughter Tomiko. Traveled all over Japan speaking until just before her death.

June 1943, age 47, published article, *Shukumei ni Katsu* (Winning Over Fate).

1946, age 50, published her biography and won Welfare Minister award, visited institutions and gave lectures.

May of 1949, published article, *Mukei no Te to Ashi* (Formless Hand and Feet).

September, 1955, published *Watakushi no Koete Kita Michi* (The Road I Traveled).

For three days, from **April 12, 1962**, age 66, gave a talk on the NHK National Radio Broadcasting System on the subject of *Go-on* (Honorable Indebtedness). It created a great sensation.

September 5, 1964, presented a statue of Kwannon Bosatsu to Kokubun Temple in Takayama City. The presentation ceremony was presided over by Mumon Yamada, President of Hanazono University.

March 19, 1968, 6:55 am, age 72, Hisako Nakamura entered the Pure Land at her home in Takayama City. Her dharma Name is *Fugyo-in Shakuni Myoshin*. Myoshin means, "Excellent Faith."

Hisako's husband
Mr. Toshio Nakamura
held a memorial exhibit
in Hisako's honor.

In Appreciation

Because of the great efforts of our pioneering *Issei* (first generation Japan-born) ministers, the Buddhist Churches of America has continued transmitting the light of the Nembutsu for eighty years now.

Through the efforts of these ministers, those of us in the United States have been able to keep in contact with fellow followers of the Nembutsu in Japan.

Reverend Bunyu Fujimura, minister emeritus of our BCA, has edited a splendid work in which he introduces us to a fellow follower of the Nembutsu in Japan. Mrs. Hisako Nakamura is a remarkable woman, who, despite lacking both of her arms and both of her legs, experienced the saving grace of the Nembutsu and experienced the great compassion of the Jodo Shinshu teaching.

This is an extremely welcomed work. I cannot express deeply enough my appreciation to Reverend Fujimura for producing this work, which I am sure will serve to deepen our understanding of the wonderful teaching left to us by Shinran Shonin.

Rev. Seigen Yamaoka, Litt.D

About the BEC

The Orange County Buddhist Church Buddhist Education Center (BEC) is the Buddhist educational program of the Orange County Buddhist Church, located in Anaheim, California. The BEC offers a variety of classes and seminars on Buddhism and Jodo Shinshu in sessions in the fall, winter, and spring. Courses range from Introduction to Buddhism and Jodo Shinshu, to textual study of Shin texts like the Larger Sutra and the Shoshinge, to related courses like Zen and Shin Buddhism, Buddhist Views of Life and Death, and Buddhist Calligraphy.

In addition to the educational program, the BEC also publishes books on Shin Buddhism. Our first publication was *Coffinman: The Journal of a Buddhist Mortician,* by Shinmon Aoki, which is a fascinating story of how one man came to meet the Shin Buddhist teachings through his work as a mortician, and how he came to sense immeasurable light in all things. Our second books are translations of the Buddhist comic book on the life of *Genza the Myokonin,* volumn one and volumn two. The BEC provided assistance in the editing of *The Buddha's Wish For the World* by Monshu

Koshin Ohtani and is in the process of editing his next book.

Future publications include a translation of a work by Hideo Yonezawa on Shin Buddhism.

Please visit our website at: www.ocbuddhist.org for information on our BEC program, Buddhist messages and notification of future publications.